GUSTAVUS ADOLPHUS COLLEGE

150 Years of Images & Stories

....
DAVE KENNEY

© 2011 by Gustavus Adolphus College

All rights reserved. No part of this book may be reproduced or transmitted in any form without written permission from Gustavus Adolphus College, 800 West College Avenue, Saint Peter, MN 56082.

•

This book was commissioned by Gustavus Adolphus College, and produced by Peg Projects, Inc., 10260 Juno Avenue North, Stillwater, Minnesota.

Project Director: Peg Guilfoyle
Designer: Cathy Spengler Design

•

Printed in Canada

•

ISBN 978-0-9602240-4-3

www.gustavus.edu

CONTENTS

Foreword · v

Preface · 1

A is for ANCESTRY · 2

B is for BENCHMARKS · 6

C is for CONVERSATION · 10

D is for DON'T · 14

E is for ELEMENTS · 18

F is for FAITH · 22

G is for GROUPS · 26

H is for HEADLINERS · 32

I is for IDEALISM · 36

J is for JOURNEY · 40

K is for KITCHENS · 44

L is for LANDMARKS · 48

M is for MORTARBOARDS · 52

Gustavus Adolphus College Timeline · 56

N is for NOTABLES · 60

O is for OCCASIONS · 64

P is for PERFORMANCE · 68

Q is for QUARTERS · 72

R is for RESILIENCE · 76

S is for STUDY · 80

T is for TOWN · 86

U is for US · 90

V is for VARSITY · 94

W is for WELCOME · 98

X is for X CHROMOSOMES · 104

Y is for Y CHROMOSOMES · 108

Z is for ZEITGEIST · 112

Å, Ä, Ö · 116

Notes · 120

Illustration Credits · 123

Index · 125

FOREWORD

We are truly grateful to those who have contributed to the richness of the Gustavus tapestry.

Reaching the 150th academic year milestone, we pause to reflect on the College's history as we look to its future of sustained excellence. To mark this milestone, the College has produced two books: *Gustavus: 150 Years of Images and Stories* and *Gustavus: 150 Years of History*. Intended to be a companion set, these books capture in very different ways the spirit and history of Gustavus Adolphus College.

More than any other Gustavus history this book, through images and stories, captures the heart of the Gustie spirit—which is easy to feel but remains difficult to define.

Of course, any attempt to tell the story of those who have lived and worked at Gustavus Adolphus College during the past 150 years will always be incomplete. Our story is one lived and told over many decades, from thousands of different viewpoints. It is a story that is still being written by every student, faculty and staff member, alum, parent, and friend of the College.

The story of Gustavus Adolphus College is not simply about recollections and nostalgia. The acts of remembering and celebrating lay a foundation for a future that we collectively imagine and must continually work to advance during our time. We must then respectively entrust the next generations to further evolve and advance that future.

As was written by former President Edgar M. Carlson in the dedication of the College's Centennial history book, we too are truly grateful, "To all those who by the single thread of their own lives have woven the fabric that is Gustavus Adolphus College."

Much has changed in 150 years for the Gustavus community. However, common themes and experiences

President Jack and Kris Ohle riding in the Gustavus Homecoming parade.

transcend the generations and connect the more than 41,000 students who have been educated at this great institution. I believe this book captures the essence of the stories that are woven into the ever-changing Gustavus tapestry.

Kris and I have been honored to be part of the Gustavus community since 2008. We have been inspired by your Gustie stories and excited to plan with you for the College's future and Sesquicentennial celebration. We look forward to sharing with you this special time in the life of the College.

Gusties will Shine!

Jack R. Ohle
President

PREFACE

I might as well come clean right now, since I'm sure I'll have to confront the issue eventually: I am *not* a Gustie. Not only that—I'm a graduate of St. Olaf, Class of '83. There. It's out in the open. I feel better now.

So how is it that an Ole has written a history of Gustavus Adolphus College? The answer to that question lies in a chain of fortuitous events that began in the spring of 2010. Gustavus put the word out that it wanted to mark its upcoming 150th anniversary by publishing a history book. My business partner, Peg Guilfoyle, and I figured that our experience in producing other institutional histories might make us a good fit for the project. We put together a proposal, crossed our fingers, and waited for a decision. To our delight, the College elected to hire us, despite my troubling association with that other Lutheran institution of higher learning in Northfield.

Over the past year and a half I've immersed myself in Gustavus, its past and present. In the process, I've become quite fond of this school on the hill. I'm impressed by its historical trajectory—the way it's grown and reinvented itself while maintaining a strong attachment to its Swedish Lutheran heritage. It's a good place to learn. It has a good story to tell.

I'm not the first person to tell this story. During the past century, two of Gustavus's most eminent faculty members, Conrad Peterson and Doniver Lund—both of the Department of History—wrote histories of this place. They approached their subject as most of their contemporaries would have, concentrating heavily on the decisions and actions of the College's presidents, administrators, and trustees. Students and faculty members received relatively little attention in the Peterson and Lund narratives.

This book is different.

It's important to keep in mind that this is just one of two volumes marking Gustavus's 150th anniversary. The second book, *Gustavus: 150 Years of History*, is a narrative history told chronologically. This one, as its title suggests, is a collection of images and stories. I invite you to read it—*absorb* it—at a leisurely pace. Start in the middle if you'd like. Choose a chapter that sounds particularly interesting—maybe "Don't" or "Us"—and move on from there. Once you get through all 27 (yes, there are 27, not 26 as you might expect), I think you'll have a good feel for this place's past and its present.

As a non-Gustie, I've needed plenty of help in making sense of the school's history, and I've been fortunate to receive enlightened and patient guidance from all the members of the College's sesquicentennial book committee including Barb Larson Taylor, Jeff Jenson, Byron Nordstrom, Steve Waldhauser, Randy Stuckey, and Judy Schultz. The research process turned out to be much easier than it might have been thanks to the efforts of Jeff Jenson and Adrianna Darden in the Gustavus Adolphus College Archives, and of their student assistants, Birgitta Johnson and Lacie Micek. Most of the people I've interviewed during the course of my research receive credit in the citations at the back of the book, but I need to acknowledge a few others who took the time to provide me with invaluable background including Renee Guittar, Brian Johnson, Chris Johnson, Virgil Jones, Tim Kennedy, Richard Leitch, Larry Owen, Jeffrey Rathlef, Matthew Swenson, and Lucy Zanders. I also am very grateful for the contributions of Stan Waldhauser, who oversaw the photography of several dozen items from the Archives, and of President Jack Ohle, whose belief in the importance of the College's history made this project possible.

With its A-to-Z (plus) format and its 500-plus images, *Gustavus: 150 Years of Images and Stories* is not a typical institutional history. The process of turning what was an intriguing but vague idea into this visually stunning volume required talents that I simply do not possess. Once again I must hand most of the credit to my frequent collaborators, project manager Peg Guilfoyle and designer Cathy Spengler. I am truly fortunate to work with two such talented colleagues, and am particularly grateful that both of them proved to be wonderful company on our long drives to and from St. Peter.

—D.K.

ANCESTRY

The shiny blue Ford F-150 that pulled up to Norelius Hall on a sweltering afternoon in late August of 2010 carried more than the assorted necessities and accessories of a freshman's existence—it bore more than a century of Gustavus **ancestry**. First-year student Jordan Almen was moving into Norelius just as her father, Ted Almen, had back in 1976. (During his time, the dorm was known as "Co-Ed.") That meant that Jordan now officially represented the fourth generation in her line of Almens to attend Gustavus. And her connection to the College went back even further than she realized.

In 1904, The Rev. Lars Gustav Almen (Jordan's great-great-grandfather) embarked on a grueling endeavor to stabilize Gustavus's shaky financial condition. For five years he traveled the state, knocking on doors and twisting arms. In the end, he raised $72,000 to create what became the college's first legitimate endowment fund.

The Rev. Almen never attended Gustavus, but all nine of his children did. One of those children, Gustav Theodore Almen 1904, was the first in a line of Gusties that included John Almen '50, Ted Almen '80, and now Jordan Almen '14.

The Almen family is just one of many with multi-generational connections to Gustavus. The names of those families live on in the current student directory and, in some cases, on campus buildings. (Vickner Hall and the Almen-Vickner Guest House, for example, are named for members of another branch of the Almen family.) Those who are born into such families may appear destined to attend the college of their forebears, but Jordan Almen insists destiny has nothing to do with it. She chose Gustavus only after visiting eight other schools.

"My mom's a Cobber from Moorhead," she says, "so she really didn't care if I went here. Dad just kind of stayed out of it. Grandma (the former Jeanette Seibel '50) waited until I decided to go here to show how excited she was. She's like a super alumna. It's funny how excited she gets about everything Gustavus."[1]

BELOW, LEFT TO RIGHT: *Ted Almen '80 helps daughter Jordan Almen '14 make the move into Norelius.*

Gustav Almen 1904

John Almen '50, editor of the 1950 Gustavian

Ted Almen '80 (far right) with the staff of the 1979 Gustavian Weekly

GENERATIONS The Almens were just one of several multi-generational Gustavus families represented on campus as the 2010–11 school year got underway.

CLOCKWISE FROM UPPER LEFT:

Lynn Regli Mauston '85, Jeff Mauston '83, Callie, Casey '14

Julie Brudwick Kjellgren '86, Grace '14, Steve Kjellgren '86

Cody '14, Charles Anderson '79, Teri Carter Anderson '79, Duncan '14

Cathy Villars Harms '85, Jennifer '14, Kelsey, Brent Harms '82

Gaylord Fernstrom '53, Erica Fernstrom '14 (granddaughter), Jeanenne Anderson Fernstrom '57

Amy '14, Frank Larson '83, William, Jennifer Strand Larson '84, Anna '11

ANCESTRY

ALUMNI The Alumni Association of Gustavus Adolphus College was established in 1890, the year of the College's first graduating class. In 1944, the association was reorganized into the Greater Gustavus Association. Over the years, Gustavus alumni have demonstrated uncommon loyalty to their alma mater, helping the Alumni Association earn 16 national awards for distinguished achievement in alumni giving.

Membership in the Alumni Association now totals more than 26,000 graduates and former students. This map, created by geography major Justin Nelson '04, shows the geographic distribution of all recorded Gustavus alumni living within the United States from 1920 to 2003. Titled "Gusties at Night," it depicts each alumna and alumnus as a spot of "light."

GUSTAVUS QUARTERLY First published in November 1944, the *Gustavus Quarterly* has kept alumni informed about the college and about each other. Updates on multigenerational families are a common feature of the magazine.

Gustavus's multi-generational appeal was firmly established by the time syndicated cartoonist Wally Falk took up the subject in 1956.[2]

LEGACIES Two multi-generational Gustavus families have left indelible marks on the college landscape. In 1980, the Eckman family of Duluth provided much of the funding for the development and construction of the campus mall. Two decades later, the Johns-Bittrich clan made possible what is now known as the Johns Family Courtyard.

 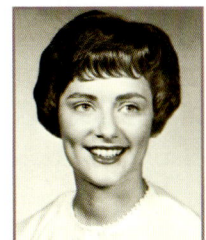

Theodore Johns '61 and Marietta Bittrich Johns '62, the primary benefactors of the Johns Family Courtyard.

The Johns family, 2001

The Eckman family, 2001

> *I find it interesting that so many Gusties have family connections here. My first roommate is a third-generation Gustie, while my other two roommates each have a younger sister at Gustavus. There are over 50 new students at Gustavus this year who are second-generation Gusties.* • Eric Wood '93[3]

Kelly Rome Johnson '84 with her daughter, Katelyn Johnson '10, a fourth-generation Gustie.

Judy Lund Erdman '57 found a creative way to commemorate her family's five-generation connection to Gustavus.

> [Some people are] literally born and bred to be Gusties . . . Generations of Blomquists, Svenssons and likes have been attending GAC for so long that something apparently gets into the blood (perhaps lutefisk is a distant relative of the salmon family) and they seem instinctively drawn to "ye old college built upon the hill." • *Gustavian Weekly,* September 21, 1979

BENCHMARKS

Many of the faculty members and other dignitaries who gathered in Christ Chapel on April 7, 1983, found it hard not to steal an occasional glance at the distinguished English professor who sat among them. Gerhard Alexis had waited for more than a quarter century for this moment to arrive. He had done more than any single person to make it happen. The ceremony in the chapel amounted to a personal and institutional triumph, and his friends and colleagues knew how much it meant to him. Phi Beta Kappa—the oldest honor society in the United States—had finally arrived at Gustavus.

It was a long time coming. Alexis had first petitioned for Gustavus to be awarded a Phi Beta Kappa chapter in 1957, convinced that an association with PBK would signal Gustavus's arrival as a top tier institution of higher learning. But that first application had failed. So had the others he prepared in the years that followed. Gustavus just didn't meet Phi Beta Kappa's standards in areas such as curriculum, library quality, and the number of faculty with Ph.D.s.

But during all those years that Alexis kept trying, Gustavus had steadily raised its standards, improved its library (thanks in large part to the efforts of a new organization, Gustavus Library Associates), and established new academic **benchmarks**. By 1980, he was convinced the College had progressed enough to make one more try. He was right. Phi Beta Kappa granted the charter, and the installation ceremony in the chapel made it official. Gustavus became the seventh college in Minnesota and one of only 234 nationwide to host a PBK chapter.

"I felt we had it coming," Alexis admitted.

At the annual Honors Day convocation a few weeks later, the persistent English professor introduced Gustavus's first Phi Beta Kappa key holders, and applauded the college for its academic progress. "I would expect," he said, "that in the long run our having the chapter will mean more and more as we increasingly understand how much is said when we state simply, 'Gustavus is a Phi Beta Kappa college.'"[1]

BELOW, LEFT TO RIGHT: *First class of students inducted into Gustavus's Phi Beta Kappa chapter, Eta of Minnesota, 1983.*
Gerhard Alexis, Department of English, 1947–83

CONDITIONS OF ADMISSION

[The student] must be able to read with tolerable facility in both languages (Swedish and English), to enter either of the regular courses, but those who do not understand Swedish may be received as special students, selecting any studies they are qualified to pursue profitably, under the direction and advice of the faculty. • **1877–78 Gustavus Catalog**

Students were forced to adapt to the College's rising academic standards as the years went on.

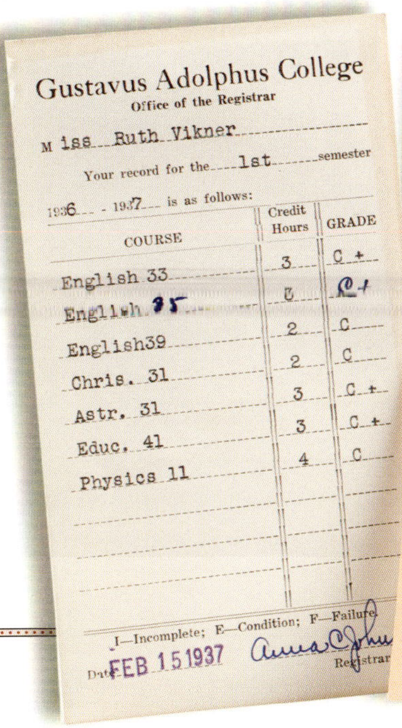

Gustavus faculty, 2008

Four Yale Ph.D.s—O.A. Winfield (philosophy), Victor Hegstrom (Greek), Conrad Peterson (history), and Joshua Larson (Swedish)—helped bolster the academic credentials of the Gustavus faculty during the 1930s.

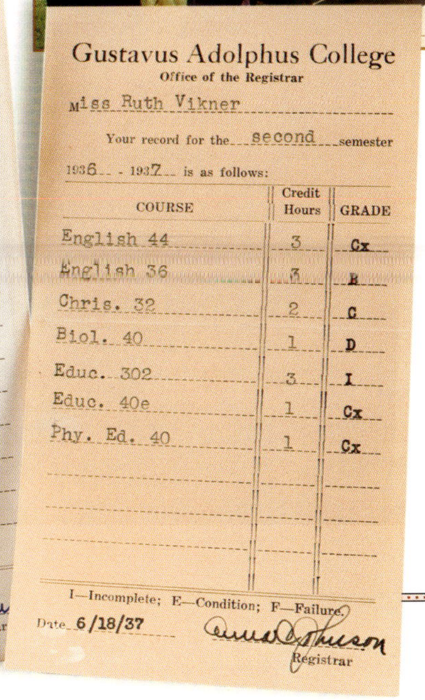

As academic standards improved, grades that were once deemed "good enough" became less and less acceptable.

B

Ph.D's are getting to be almost as plentiful on the Gustavus campus as sidewalks.

• • •

Gustavian Weekly,
October 14, 1947

BENCHMARKS

CURRICULUM The curriculum at Gustavus Adolphus College has become more rigorous over the years.

Gustavus Ladies' Summer Sewing School, about 1880

DEPARTMENTS.

The Collegiate Department.

This Department offers to the student a thorough and practical course, combining in just proportions the classics and the sciences. Besides the subjects usually studied in American Colleges, prominence is given to Swedish history and literature, and to Christian doctrine.

Every student who has completed the full course of studies and has satisfied the Faculty and Board of Directors as to his good character and maturity of mind, will receive the degree of BACHELOR OF ARTS.

By 1890, Gustavus had expanded its curriculum sufficiently to grant its first A.B. degrees.

Whatever we do, let us do it well. Let the quality of our work be good—this will recommend our work and we cannot help but go forward. • Eric Norelius to William K. Frick, May 9, 1887[2]

During its first two decades, Gustavus was a college in name only.

On the 15th of May, 1890, the institution sent forth its first graduates, and, conferring upon them the title A.B., became G.A. College not merely in name but in reality. It now stands on equal footing with other colleges, and as such, second to none in the state. •
Annual Messenger [first student newspaper], 1891

In the mid-1910s, the college introduced a new system of majors and minors to accommodate its growing curriculum.

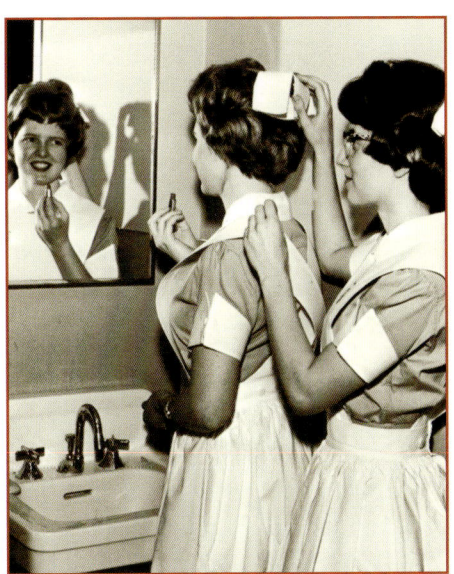

The post-war years brought the addition of new academic programs including home economics (above) and nursing (right), which were designed specifically for young women. Only the nursing program survived past the 1950s.

In this day of sputniks ... and added emphasis on education the once fashionable "gentleman C" seems to be taking, and not "so slowly but surely," a back seat to what one might call an "aristocratic A." • Gustavian Weekly, February 26, 1960

The teachers' loads have been heavy, requirements for study and standards of achievement have been high. For the most part, those standards have been set by the students themselves through the competition which they have offered one another. That is as it should be. • President Edgar Carlson '30, 1947[3]

Members of the Class of '66 were among the first students to attend Gustavus under what administrators touted as the "new curriculum." The changes, introduced in the early 1960s, included the introduction of four-course semesters and a new January Term.

The first group of Curriculum II graduates, 1989. Curriculum II offers students the option of taking an integrated group of courses—in sequence—during their four years at Gustavus.

Being just a few weeks into my final semester at Gustavus ... I look back at all I have done and learned through Curriculum II and know that it has been a great fit for me. The Curriculum II program was a huge part of what originally attracted me to Gustavus, and it has certainly lived up to my expectations. • Adam Strand '10

CONVERSATION

Many of the 600 or so first-year students gathered in the cafeteria for the 1976 freshman banquet were intrigued—or maybe confused. The man who had just begun talking to them did not fit the mold of a small midwestern liberal arts college professor. He had a dark handlebar-ish moustache, big horn-rimmed glasses, and spoke in a drawl that indicated he did not come from anywhere near Minnesota.

"Welcome to the conversation!" he declared.

Strange way to start a speech.

The man with the moustache was Larry Owen, a 13-year veteran of Gustavus's Department of English. He had come to the banquet to deliver what, at first blush, seemed to be a simple message: "Come on in—let's talk." "Let's talk," he repeated. But talk about what? With whom? Owen's advice was to start a conversation with a professor:

"Go to Professor Charles Hamrum and say: 'I want to get to know dragonflies.' If you do that on the first Monday of your freshman year you might, if you're lucky, start a conversation that will last four years.

"Go to Professor Bill Levis and say: 'Tell me what Australian playwrights are doing these days.'

"Go to Professor William Dean and say: 'What does love have to do with physics?'"

"The conversation," as Owen readily admitted, was a metaphor—a vessel capable of containing any and all pursuits of knowledge and understanding. It could happen in a dorm room, the chapel, the caf, the Flame. It could involve friends, profs, musical scores, dissected frogs, batted baseballs. "Come on in—let's talk," he repeated. "And if the talk won't do it, we might sing, or dance, or make a poem, or walk a path where wild raspberries grow."

In the years that followed, other freshman orientation speakers picked up the theme and urged first-year Gusties to join "the conversation." Owen kept delivering the message too. "A few students have said to me in their senior year that they remembered that talk, and they thanked me for it," he said. "So I guess it did work on some of them."[1]

Larry Owen

Is it not true that there is more to an education and background than just cramming for a midterm test or paraphrasing a term paper? It is through [personal relationships] with the college faculty that the student can seek out good sound advice.
• *Gustavian Weekly,* October 26, 1956

During Gustavus's first century, most faculty members preferred to confine their interactions with students to the classroom.

A "students-only" gathering at the Canteen, early 1960s.

It would appear that students are content to sit in the Canteen and watch TV while they nurse their coffee, and that the professors are only mildly disturbed to sit in their corner of the cafeteria and munch nickel donuts.
• *Gustavian Weekly,* November 19, 1965

An essential part of every class is, of course, the professor . . . their droll humor (jokes, if you will), their characteristic phrases, their absent-mindedness, even their lectures. [We] can safely say (with mixed feelings) when we survey the supply of knowledge gleaned from our years in college, "We owe it all to them!" • 1943 *Gustavian*

In what's become a popular teaching technique in recent years, Karl Larson, Department of Health and Exercise Science, moves his classroom outdoors, 2010.

Seán Easton, Department of Classics, engages students in the classroom, 2009.

C CONVERSATION

IMPACT In 2003, the *Gustavian Quarterly* asked alumni to share their thoughts about faculty members "who had the most profound or lasting impact on their lives." Many of the Gustavians who responded to that request reflected on how their favorite teachers enjoyed engaging in what Larry Owen called "the conversation."

George Forell, Department of Christianity, 1947–56

Ron Christenson, Department of Political Science, 1969–98

Once you got to know him, it was not difficult to turn an oral exam into a very engaging conversation in which Ron actually did most of the talking.
• Ron Carlson '81[2]

There were times when [Forell] stood on the desk to prove a point. Many times our arguments carried over from the classroom to the Canteen—with other students following us. • Vern Bergstrom '51[1]

I was privileged to have Professor Lindemann as my adviser and from time to time would climb the rickety stairs to sit with him in his cluttered, windowless North Hall office. We would smoke at each other and talk of myriad things—World War I airplanes and A.E. Hosman and women and German beer. He sensed in me an inclination to doubt, to challenge, and he encouraged it. And he noted a precocious cynicism and sought to discourage it. • Jerry Thorson '60[3]

J. W. R. Lindemann, Department of English, 1948–60

Helen Baumgartner, Department of Music, 1966–2004

I think the single most important lesson I took away from Gustavus was that education is a whole-person enterprise, not just an intellectual challenge. One manifestation of this that particularly stands out was my weekly piano lesson with Helen Baumgartner. We always started with a few minutes' chat about how I was doing, really doing, and at the end of the lesson she always sent me off by wishing me well—either to hang in there or to carry on cheerfully—on whatever it was we'd talked about before turning to music. • Erika Lucast '00[4]

What I want to know is what [my students'] questions are. That is where learning starts—for them and for me. The genius of the young lies not in what they know . . . but in what they want to know. And from the students' questions come the teacher's stimulation to learn. • Will Freiert, Department of Classics, 1972–2010[5]

I'm always teaching information in the classroom, but I'm not so concerned that my students remember specific facts. Imparting information is only effective if it helps students develop the capacity to look at life very broadly and from different perspectives, to think things through, and to understand and apply ideas. • Linnea Wren, Department of Art and Art History, 1976–present[6]

I try to let my students know that I care about them. If they know that, they will work hard for you. . . . I want to know the students I'm interacting with. I want it to be a two-way street. • John Lammert, Department of Biology, 1982–present[7]

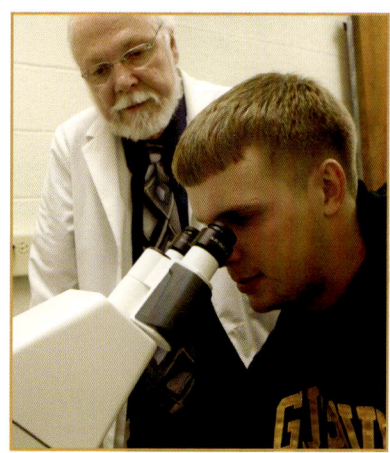

Because students are not satisfied with easy answers to [philosophical] questions, I am continually challenged to think about new ways to explain and justify the study of philosophy. Students also regularly provide me with unusual readings of a book I've read dozens of times before.
• Lisa Heldke '82, Department of Philosophy, 1988–present[8]

D DON'T

Back in 1891, Gustavus President Matthias Wahlstrom had delivered a sermon that appealed to his student listeners. "We **don't** expect that you shall be saints," he told them, "but we do surely *not* expect to find in you those who work all the mischief they can."[1] Wahlstrom was known for his kind heart and willingness to indulge youthful exuberance, but even his patience would have been tested by the events that occurred during Halloween week, 1934.

Several years earlier, an enterprising businessman named Hilding Nelson (better known as "Skoning") had opened a small diner and store on the college hill, just a few steps from the new men's dormitory (later known as Uhler Hall). Skoning served hamburgers, ice cream, and fountain drinks, and kept a ready supply of student-pleasing goodies—candy, cigarettes, maybe even under-the-counter hooch if you knew how to ask. His shack did not lack for customers.

But when students returned to campus in the fall of 1934, they were chagrined to find that Skoning's had closed. The shack was locked and empty. And to the residents of the adjacent men's dorm, it posed a challenge.

On the night of November 1, several dozen Gustavus men rocked Skoning's shack off its foundation and sent it rolling down the hill. Although the college handbook contained no prohibitions against shack-tipping, authorities in St. Peter frowned on vandalism. One of the participants was arrested, and the rest of the perpetrators—including a future St. Peter minister, Millard Ahlstrom '34—were required to pay $5.50 each in restitution.

In the months and years that followed, the "shack incident" assumed near mythic status among would-be rule-breakers on campus. The 1935 *Gustavian* recast the story as an epic poem. It ended with an admonition:

The moral of this tale, my dears
Is clear as it can be:
Don't *do it again another year.*
It isn't safe for thee.[2]

RULES & REGULATIONS

In the college's early years, prank-loving Gusties reveled in testing the rule-quoting administration's patience. They had several favorite targets including the daily chapel service and the small, but tempting, menagerie of campus animals.

Gustavus do's and don'ts—1885 edition.

The authorities at our college, in some past time, took measures for safeguarding the morals of the students by making some very wise rules in regard to dancing, pool playing, and the use of liquor and tobacco. At the present time not even an attempt is made to enforce these rules, which could and ought to be enforced.

- *Gustavian Weekly,* May 1, 1923

Cartoonist Eben Lawson captured the rule-breaking spirit of the 1920s.

Chapel in the Auditorium

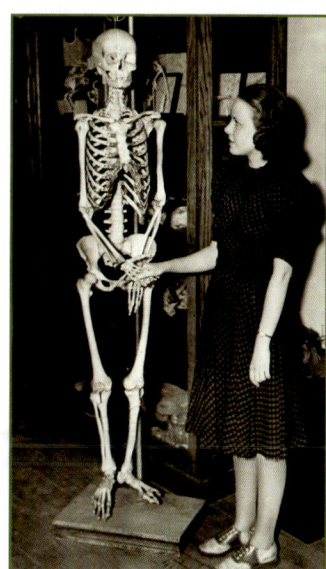

Dr. Uhler's "extinguished" chapel guest—property of the Department of Biology.

Where, but in chapel, could one catch the eye of faculty, administration and student body in one fell swoop? [The pranks I remember] include: hidden alarm clocks ringing; paper clips on piano strings; flying pigeons; chains to lock doors so students could not get in; chains to lock students in so they could not get out; a December chapel where, five minutes after the service had started, an item of feminine lingerie with the message "Merry Christmas" fluttered from the ceiling and remained suspended over the podium; and much earlier, so the story goes, a skeleton appearing when Dr. Uhler was in charge. After taking note of his "extinguished" guest, he continued the service.

- Doniver Lund, Department of History, 1987[3]

The cow that custodian Hans Amundson kept in a field close to campus was a frequent victim of pranksters. "Amundson's Ko" repeatedly showed up in unexpected places including the second floor of Old Main. Other targets of campus mischief included a rooster belonging to Swedish professor Karl Kilander ("Kilander's Tupp") and President Peter Mattson's goat.

DON'T

DON'T LINGER
"No male student is permitted to call at [the] Ladies Dormitory, go walking or accompany any Coed unless he shall have a standing of or above ninety."
• *Gustavian Weekly,* September 18, 1920

DON'T DANCE
Dear Editor:
In response to your editorial of last week about dancing at G.A., the Rundstrom girls want to let you know that we stand strongly behind you. ¶ In view of the fact that the majority of Gustavians do dance, will dance, and are dancing, we would like to see our college move ahead with the modern trend of thought.
• *Gustavian Weekly,* November 12, 1954

DON'T PARK HERE
The no parking areas are clearly marked and any car that is illegally parked in one of these areas will be tagged and the owner asked to report to the Personnel Office. A person will be charged a dollar for the first offense and for additional violations be charged progressively more—the second offense two dollars, etc., ad infinitum. • *Gustavian Weekly,* October 16, 1953

DON'T WALK ON THE GRASS
When we encounter a new series of barriers blocking our favorite shortcut, in our last dash to make a 7:50 class some morning in the near future, let's not consider them part of an obstacle course imposed to bring track hopefuls extra conditioning. • *Gustavian Weekly,* March 29, 1949

DON'T SMOKE
President Carlson made a request at the beginning of the school year asking that there be no smoking in the classroom buildings. Last week it was necessary for him to re-emphasize that request. Why should that be necessary? • *Gustavian Weekly,* April 29, 1947

DON'T DRINK
The recent statement from the administration concerning drinking in the dormitories is the most encouraging step we have seen recently in the disciplinary area at GA. The posted notice [stipulates] immediate expulsion for anyone found drinking intoxicants within the dorm. • *Gustavian Weekly,* April 30, 1965

DON'T SKATEBOARD
Security has been asking people to skateboard [off campus] in the interest of the safety of the skateboarders and pedestrians. Dale Haack, the director of Physical Plant, said, "If someone's hurt, it comes back to the college in a negative way." • *Gustavian Weekly,* October 4, 1991

DON'T FORGET YOUR CLOTHES
Ma Young wasn't too happy about [a streaker's appearance in the cafeteria] . . . until she started thinking about the expressions on the cooks' faces and then couldn't suppress a "boys will be boys" smile. • *Gustavian Weekly,* March 15, 1974

ELEMENTS

Generations of Gustavians have learned through experience that winter achieves its true potential on the hill overlooking St. Peter. Over the years, ice, snow, wind, and gravity have occasionally combined to create conditions that turn even the most poised student or faculty member into a human luge. The hill "knows nothing of Ph.D.s and the like," observed a *Gustavian Weekly* reporter in 1930. "It only knows that a middle-aged [professor] with a funny brown bag, and spectacles, would make a fine toboggan."[1]

Winter can be harsh on the hill, but those willing to overlook inconveniences such as frozen eyelashes and numb extremities often learn to take advantage of the **elements**. After all, a college on a hill does have certain advantages when it comes to winter recreation.

For more than 100 years, the hill sloping away from Old Main has attracted daredevils and fun-lovers of all ages. In the College's early years, student "coasters" hopped on toboggans and bobsleds and shot down the hill with little regard for oncoming traffic. The College briefly banned coasting in 1921 after the oldest son of Swedish professor Karl Kilander was seriously injured in a collision with a passing automobile, but it relented a few years later, to the delight of many restless students.[2]

By the early 1970s, coasting had given way to a new form of winter fun—traying. No longer was it necessary for a student to invest in a toboggan or sled. A cafeteria tray worked just fine. "It is a well-known fact that most trays are stolen from Mrs. Young's cafeteria," a reporter with the *Weekly* observed. "If you would like to participate, but you are not a rip-off artist, just borrow one from somebody with some guts."[3] Today traying remains a popular winter diversion at Gustavus, although it is no longer considered larcenous. The Gustavus Dining Service now lends out trays with a plea that they eventually be returned.

BELOW, LEFT TO RIGHT: *Patrick Perish '12, Anna Yost '12, Katie Asfeld '12, Sophia Ogren-Dehn '11, and Erin Simon '12 ride a "train" of trays down the Rundstrom Hall hill, 2010.*

1950s

Old Main's icy steps seemed to afford the greatest entertainment. A group of our very courteous gentlemen stationed themselves below the steps, watching with evident amusement the frantic efforts of a herd of their fellow students to propel themselves down to the comparative safety of the sidewalk. Several gave up the attempt entirely, and merely slid down clutching wildly at the air during the process.

• *Gustavian Weekly,* January 9, 1934

E

Winter at Gustavus: The time of year when you think about the colleges down south you applied to.

• • •

1973 *Gustavian*

1910s

And while I'm thinking about it, where exactly is my car? I had a blue Honda but overnight all the cars in the [Norelius parking] lot seem to have been transformed into white driftmobiles. Probably someone's idea of a funny prank.

• 1984 *Gustavian*

ELEMENTS

This is the time of the year when we always feel an unusual depth of gratitude to the pioneer fathers of Gustavus Adolphus College for placing it high upon the hilltop overlooking the beautiful valley below. The scene across the valley yonder these days, with the trees beginning the annual colorful autumn festival, is one to strike a universal aesthetic sense within the undergraduate's soul, as well as within the soul of anyone else. • *Gustavian Weekly,* October 12, 1937

And autumn, too, has come. ¶ Turning leaves on Hill and Valley, dashing winds at play in hollow and gutter, the earthy smell of burning grasses, all unmindful, evidence of the coming. The landscape startles. Far and near, the faint flushes of reds and golds greet the eyes. Tints of indistinct purples, hues of oranges and browns, and shades of greens blend in harmony unconsciously bringing to mind thoughts of the Giver.
• *Gustavian Weekly,* October 11, 1927

Chaotic patterns
of autumn leaves create a colorful mosaic
on the path.

Along the way
Flower blossoms,
Bright in the moist air,
Decorate a wrought-iron fence.

A subtle
Hint of Winter
Is in the breeze
As the soft earth
Absorbs my footsteps.

• • •

Gretchen Koehler, Department of Health and Exercise Science, 1992[4]

*Each morning
the nimble air said:
"Winter is over,
no budding wood or blooming gardens
here on the prairie:
only throbbing spring,
its light restlessness
playfully roaming
across the rolling country,
impulsive like a big puppydog,
stopping to sniff burning grass,
to listen to a woodpecker
hammer away at a crooked elm,
and then trot on,
until, at the horizon,
spring meets sky, pale sunshine,
swift clouds—
a big puppy pawing you
then lying down to be petted."*

• Elmer Suderman, Department of English, 1974

Yes, spring has come to Gustavus . . . and the flood. The alma mater may be outclassed by "Anchors Aweigh." But, before we change our tune, let's just hope. Let's hope that we some day return to the campus to find sidewalks which remain above water, and roads which do not give the impression of that first ride on the roller-coaster . . . perhaps even surfaced roadways. • *Gustavian Weekly,* March 31, 1950

Once again spring has joyfully made its entrance on our beloved campus and all optimistic females are turning their faces and beautiful forms to the south, scanning the skies for the first brave sunbeam that forces its way to earth. The time has arrived for the girls to don, or should we say undon, their sunbathing attire and the boys to refocus their high-power telescopes and drag out the cameras. • *Gustavian Weekly,* March 25, 1955

FAITH

Gustavus had begun as a school of the church, located within the walls of a church. Its first home, in Red Wing, was a tiny Lutheran church built by some of Minnesota's earliest Swedish immigrants. Its second home was the log cabin that originally served as the East Union Evangelical Lutheran Church. But when the school relocated to St. Peter in 1876, it no longer had a dedicated worship space. It wasn't until 1905 that Gustavus created a place specifically designed to nurture **faith**—a chapel in the newly constructed Auditorium.

The chapel in the Aud served Gustavus well for more than four decades, but by the early 1950s, it had lost its luster. It was too small to accommodate the post-war explosion in enrollment, and was serving as a frequent venue for talent shows and pep rallies. "It just doesn't seem right to worship in an auditorium where so many secular activities are carried on," Donald Sisson '56 lamented, echoing the feelings of many students.[1]

In 1955 four students representing Gustavus's Lutheran Student Association (LSA) attended the annual meeting of the Lutheran Minnesota Conference to make the case for a new college chapel. It was a pivotal moment. The Conference responded to their presentation by approving a $450,000 fundraising campaign.

With President Edgar Carlson leading the way, the Gustavus community rallied behind the slogan, "A College Church for a Church College." In the campaign's first few weeks, 175 students spoke at 210 churches, appealing for donations.[2] As the money trickled in, plans took shape. The design that emerged envisioned a 114-foot square topped by a towering spire—a modern chapel that, in Carlson's words, would "express the faith which is the center of Christian higher education."[3]

On January 7, 1962, Gustavus's new Christ Chapel was formally dedicated. For Carlson—a teacher, administrator, and ordained minister—it was "a dream realized." "[The dedication] was a special thrill for those of us who had already lived with [the new chapel] for several years while it was being conceived and taking form," Carlson wrote. "Already it has left its stamp on many of us. . . . If you give it a chance, it will leave its mark on you, too."[4]

BELOW: *Christ Chapel dedication, 1962*

Chapel services in the Auditorium.

Friends, do you realize the presence and nearness of God during those moments of spiritual growth? Are you acting accordingly? When you enter the Chapel, will you not take your seat immediately, and put aside all books, papers and pencils, cease from whispering or loud talking, and enter whole-heartedly into our devotional exercises, to refresh your souls, by singing praises to God from whom all blessings flow? • *Gustavian Weekly,* April 17, 1923

For me, the Gustavus experience was seeing life through those holy windows. We didn't look through colorful stained glass recounting old Bible stories, because we were eyewitnesses to God's activity right outside. The scripture and song inside Christ Chapel filtered through the windows to our academics and our relationships. The glass was the lens that sanctified the campus. • Nancy L. H. Brown '79[5]

Postcard view of the newly completed Christ Chapel.

I can only urge you to preserve this empty place in the daily schedule for worship. If you do not, your life will become increasingly harassed and hectic as you try to cover up the embarrassment of having an empty heart that has lost the presence of God. • Robert Esbjornson '41, Department of Religion, 2007[6]

Gustavus's longest-tenured chaplains: Richard Elvee, 1962–2000 (left); Brian Johnson '80, 1996–2011 (right).

FAITH

THIRD PATH Gustavus's relationship with religion and the Lutheran Church has evolved over the past 150 years. During its first century, Gustavus relied heavily on spiritual and financial support from what was known as the Minnesota Conference of the Lutheran Augustana Synod. During the past 50 years, those bonds have loosened as the Lutheran Church itself has reorganized. Today many members of the college community see Gustavus not as a sectarian or non-sectarian institution, but as a college committed to what Religion Professor Darrell Jodock calls a "third path"— an approach that "takes religious diversity seriously enough to engage and struggle with it."[7] The evolution of Gustavus's religious identity can be traced in the words of its leaders and its publications.

1876

You must either adopt the Christian or Bible system and acknowledge a personal God, who is the Creator, Law-Giver, the Governor, and the Judge of the universe, or rejecting this, you have nothing. . . . Now we do not hesitate to profess that we are Christian. • Eric Norelius, Gustavus founder[8]

1881

Man is a religious being, and any scheme of education which neglects to provide for this fact is necessarily defective. Intellectual and religious culture must go hand in hand to make education productive of good.

• 1881–82 Gustavus Catalog

1907

The aim of our colleges is, then, I take it, to serve our Swedish Lutheran Church in the development of true Christian characters.

• Peter Mattson 1892, Gustavus president, 1904–11[9]

1933

The Christian college has a definite program of high ideals and aims. It teaches faith in and reverence for God. . . . It has arranged its courses and programs so that spiritual growth will be an important part of the development of the student. • O. J. Johnson, Gustavus president, 1913–42[10]

During the early 1930s, future Gustavus president Edgar Carlson '30 and classmates Emmer Engberg '30, Daniel Friberg '30, and Russell Nelson '30 logged thousands of miles in the "Missionary Ford" spreading the Gospel throughout the upper Midwest.

MEMBER — Gustavus Adolphus Missionary Society — 1934-35 — "Send Out The Light"

This mural in the original Folke Bernadotte Memorial Library portrayed Jesus Christ at the center of a variety of campus scenes. It was painted by Don Gregory, head of the Gustavus Department of Art.

The Gustavus Proclaim Band leads in praise and worship, 2009.

1961

The fullest possible development of the mind and its dedication to the God we know in Jesus Christ and to the welfare of all mankind is the goal of education at Gustavus Adolphus College. • Edgar Carlson '30, Gustavus president, 1944–68[11]

1970

Religion is the diamond on which are cut the many facets of Gustavus life, that is to say, we consider God, from whom all things come forth and to whom all things return, to be the ground and source of our life. • 1970 Gustavus Catalog

1984

Gustavus students see campus religious life differently, according to the emphasis they have established for themselves. In this variety are diverse religious philosophies. • 1984 Gustavus Catalog

1988

Colleges like Gustavus that refuse to draw the line between the secular and the sacred have a very special place in the world. They are important because they provide the setting for understanding the complex moral, social and civic problems of our time—an understanding that can be found in very few places. • John Kendall '49, Gustavus president, 1981–91[12]

2008

[At Gustavus] we have clarity that Christian faith is central to the identity and life of this institution. . . . As a college of the Church we do not expect conformity to specific religious traditions, but we encourage an honest exploration of religious faith and seek to foster an understanding of Christian perspectives in our lives. • Jack Ohle, Gustavus president, 2008–present[13]

2010

Gustavus Adolphus College is a church-related, residential liberal arts college firmly rooted in its Swedish and Lutheran heritage. . . . The College aspires to be a community of persons from diverse backgrounds who respect and affirm the dignity of all people. It is a community where a mature understanding of the Christian faith and lives of service are nurtured and students are encouraged to work toward a just and peaceful world. • 2010–11 Gustavus Catalog

GROUPS

As the maze of tables takes shape on Eckman Mall, Lacey Squier '11 surveys the scene with the eye of a practiced veteran. Three years earlier, as a first-year student, she had made a point of attending this same event—the fall Involvement Fair. She had been a dancer in high school, but knew she wouldn't be dancing at Gustavus. She wanted to find another extracurricular activity to fill the resulting void, but she didn't know what that might be. So she went to the Involvement Fair—and went a little crazy.

"I was really excited," she admits. "By the end of the day, I had signed up for seven different organizations."

Lacey didn't end up joining all those **groups**, but she did join two—the Campus Activities Board (CAB) and the student radio station, KGSM. CAB, with its responsibility for a broad range of activities including concerts, movies, and major events like homecoming, turned out to be a particularly good fit. Now, in her senior year, she's serving as the group's co-president.

This year's Involvement Fair gives Lacey a chance to play the elder stateswoman, to stand back and watch as her CAB colleagues try out a new soft-sell approach with potential recruits. "We don't want to be so heavily pressuring people," she says. "Our goal is let the people who are interested know what's available to them and let them know that they can come and hang out for a meeting or two and get a feel for what it's like." When a freshman begins hovering near the CAB table, she abandons her observer role and draws him into a five-minute conversation about his interests and whether the CAB would be a good match.

Activity fairs like this have been taking place at Gustavus since at least the mid-1980s. Today, with more than 100 groups officially recognized by the College, the ability to sample from a smörgåsbord of activities has never been more crucial. "This is just so convenient," Lacey says, gesturing to the hubbub on the mall. "It made a world of difference to me."[1]

BELOW: *Lacey Squier '11 oversees the Campus Activities Board table at the 2010 fall Involvement Fair.*

DEBATE AND ORATORY Of all the extracurricular activities that have enriched campus life over the years, none can claim as long and enduring a legacy as forensics. The debate and oratory tradition at Gustavus dates back to at least the 1890s. During the first decade of the 20th century, when intercollegiate sports were banned on campus, the exploits of the debate and oratory teams were an especially welcome source of school pride. The Gustavus forensics program has continued to enjoy great success ever since. In recent years, it has reestablished itself as a national power, scoring four consecutive top-20 showings in the American Forensic Association National Individual Events Tournament.

Competitors in debate and oratory were the "big men (and, occasionally, women) on campus" of their day. In 1902, a special train carried about 250 Gustavians to Northfield for the first state oratorical contest—an event that seems to have established the college's black and gold colors, school songs, and spirit yells.[2]

Athletics and forensics represent in a sense the two extremities in extracurricular activities. The one mostly physical stamina; the other mental acuity. Both are necessary factors in life. • *Gustavian Weekly,* March 12, 1923

Gustavus hosted a series of annual debates with Oxford and other British universities beginning in the late 1920s. The series was interrupted during World War II, but resumed briefly during the 1950s.

In recent years, Gustavus's forensics program has reestablished itself as a national powerhouse, scoring top-20 finishes in four consecutive American Forensic Association National Individual Events Tournaments and a Pi Kappa Delta national championship in 2010.

G GROUPS

1952 Student Senate

Are you robbing yourself without being aware of it? You might be if you don't take advantage of what the many worthwhile organizations and clubs at Gustavus have to offer. ¶ In these clubs you can meet more friends, gain more of an all-around education and in general have a good time while doing something worthwhile for yourself and others.
• *Gustavian Weekly,* December 14, 1951

Gustavus Aquatic League, 1943

Every student owes it to himself to select certain lines of outside interest at the beginning of his college career and then deliberately endeavor to make a mark in at least one of them. . . . By participation in various kinds of student organizations, one can more speedily and accurately discover one's particular aptitudes and can thus make a better and surer choice of one's life work. • *Gustavian Weekly,* January 8, 1921

"Drama on Parade," a student-produced program from the campus-based radio studio of KYSM, Mankato, 1940.[3]

1993 edition of the Gustavus Sauna Society, established two years earlier by a pair of Gusties from Hibbing, Minn.[4]

You've got to be a special kind of individual to play IMs. Not too big, not too small, not playing a varsity sport at the time, willing to give up eating dinner at the usual time and taking a chance on missing that certain someone you always look for in the café. You can be a freak or just a high school jock with a carryover complex and like to get into fights when things aren't going your way in the game, and then have to apologize for almost hitting some guy and then being labeled as a jerk for the rest of the semester.
• 1975 *Gustavian*

IM broomball, 2010

IM dodgeball, 2009

IM hockey, 1975

IM softball, 1970s

So all you girls head to the cafeteria—go to the canteen—EAT! Become a [powderpuff football] hog! Stick those ends in the air and eat the dust; toss the pigskin for at least an hour a day and shoot the bull about last Saturday's football game. It's a sure sign of a good hog and [coach Jocko Nelson] will love you for it. • *Gustavian Weekly,* September 26, 1969

A novel football game between two teams of Gustavus women (the "Heavies" vs. the "Leans") produced national headlines in 1923.[5]

Gustavus women returned to the gridiron in the 1970s with a series of powderpuff football games pitting freshman-sophomore "Babes" against junior-senior "Old Mares."[6]

29

GROUPS

Gustavian Weekly *staff, early 1920s*

Headliners

Marion Nestle, an expert on food and nutrition policy, has just delivered the opening lecture at Gustavus's 2010 Nobel Conference, and she's famished. For the past 15 minutes, she has graciously fielded questions from a procession of admirers lined up at the base of the speaker's platform inside Lund Arena, but her patience is running thin. She got in late the night before, missed breakfast, and now is running late for a luncheon being held in the Three Crowns Room. Luckily for her, one of her student hosts, Sam Frings '12, is there to whisk her away.

"Are you hungry?" Sam asks as they thread their way through the crowd.

"Boy, am I!"

Sam escorts her guest to the luncheon and sits next to her at the head table. Then, to Sam's delight and amazement, they start talking—truly talking. Nestle, the kickoff speaker at this gathering of world-renowned **headliners**, wants to know who Sam is and what she plans to do with her life. (She's an education major and hopes to become a teacher.) The conversation continues later when Sam and two other student hosts take Nestle on a walking tour of St. Peter.

Gustavus instituted the Nobel Conference in 1965 with the aim of bringing together some of the world's greatest thinkers to discuss some of the most critical issues of the day. Over the years the conference has delivered a side benefit: it's allowed many Gustavus students to interact directly with those same speakers. Not all Nobel Conference participants are as willing as Marion Nestle to spend time with inexperienced college students, but many prove to be charming company.

As this year's conference continues, Sam and her fellow student hosts get a chance to spend additional quality time with several other speakers including Cary Fowler and Linda Bartoshuk. "We expected to maybe talk to them a little bit and ask them whether they needed coffee or something," Sam says, "but they really accommodated us. They took the chance to get to know all the students."[1]

BELOW LEFT: *2010 Nobel Conference presenter Marion Nestle and her student host, Sam Frings '12.*

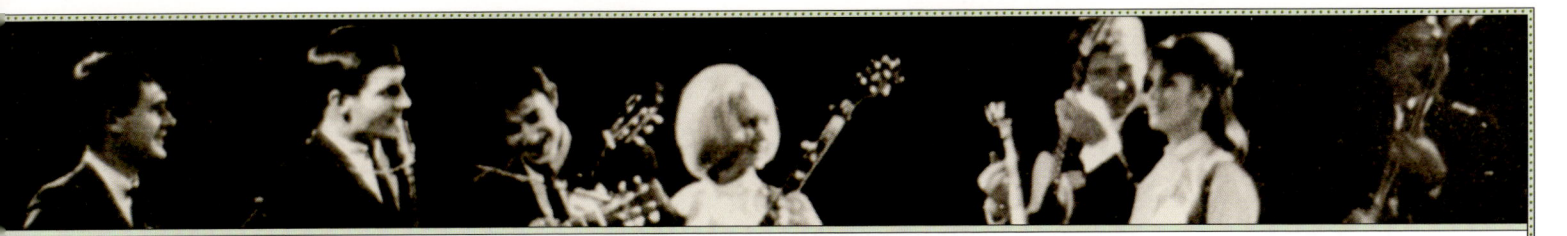

The Christy Minstrels, 1964

The visit of more than 20 Nobel prize winners to the Gustavus Adolphus campus this weekend is a notable event for all Minnesota. It places emphasis not only on the intellectual attainments of America but also on the steady cultural and academic growth of the St. Peter college. • *Mankato Free Press,* **May 3, 1963**

Gustavus's association with the Nobel Foundation began in 1963 when 26 Nobel laureates came to campus for the dedication of Gustavus's Alfred Nobel Hall of Science. That gathering led to the establishment in 1965 of the annual Nobel Conferences at Gustavus. Most of the conferences have explored the physical and social dimensions of scientific knowledge. More than 60 Nobel laureates have participated in the Nobel Conferences since their inception in 1965.

It is rare to have the opportunity to participate in a conference in which high school, college and university students of such diverse backgrounds are brought together in such a wonderful environment for discussion of topics of vital interest to mankind as has been developed at Gustavus College.

• Norman Borlaug, 1971 Peace Prize winner[2]

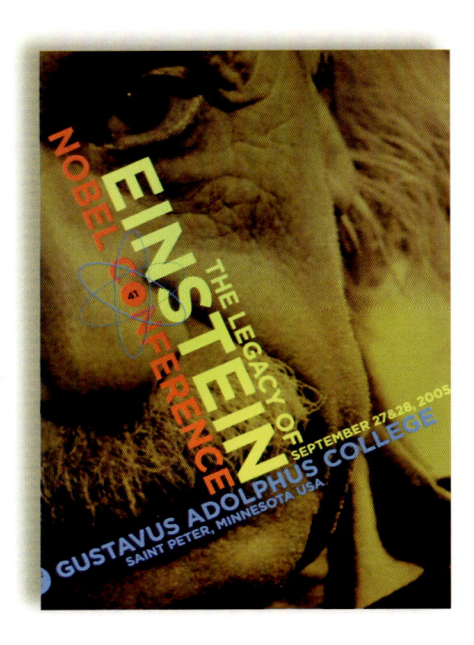

Another two dozen Nobel laureates have visited Gustavus outside the confines of the Nobel Conferences.

LEFT TO RIGHT: Toni Morrison, winner of the 1993 Nobel Prize for Literature, spoke at the Gustavus Library Associates' Author Day in 1997. 1986 Peace Prize winner Elie Wiesel delivered Gustavus's commencement address in 1994. Derek Walcott, winner of the 1992 Nobel Prize for Literature, participated in a three-week residency at Gustavus in 2010.

HEADLINERS

In 1900, William Jennings Bryan brought his presidential campaign to St. Peter, giving many Gustavus students their first opportunity to hear a speaker of national stature.

Former British Prime Minister Clement Attlee was one of the first world leaders to visit Gustavus. During his stay in 1959, he joined President Edgar Carlson in the groundbreaking for the College's new chapel.

> Following [Sandburg's] lecture, a reception was held at Rundstrom Hall for the famous poet, who endeared himself to all the students by shaking hands and chatting informally with each one.
> • **Gustavian Weekly,** February 24, 1942

Poet Carl Sandburg, 1942

Filmmaker Spike Lee, 1992

Activist Angela Davis, 2006

Broadcast journalist Lisa Ling, 2007

> Even Dr. Carlson was the victim of [the dummy Charlie McCarthy's] wit. We wonder to this day if our prexy really does know who Miles Standish was.
> • *Gustavian Weekly,* **October 6, 1950**

Ventriloquist Edgar Bergen and Charlie McCarthy (with President Edgar Carlson), 1950

The Smothers Brothers, 1963

Robert Merrill, operatic baritone, 1971

Johnny Mathis, 1965

> With the exception of Mike Love's bare-chested strutting, it seems the Beach Boys no longer earn encores; they simply endure them. Even though the concert was something less than an artistic success, a good time was had by all.
> • *Gustavian Weekly,* **November 9, 1973**

Al Jardine of the Beach Boys, 1974

Ben Folds, 2008

In 1968, a trio of singer-songwriters named Denver, Boise and Johnson performed for the first time at Gustavus. Two of its members—John Denver and Michael Johnson—made multiple appearances as solo artists at Gustavus during the early 1970s. Johnson continued to return to campus for concerts in the decades that followed.

35

IDEALISM

As students trudged out of the cafeteria on their way to Monday morning classes on November 15, 2010, they encountered an unusual sight—a small band of fellow Gusties, scattered outside the caf entrance, with bleary eyes and rumpled clothes. Some sat cross-legged on the floor, looking up expectantly as people walked by. Others hovered nearby, eyeing breakfast trays on their slow journey to the dishwasher. Clearly they were hungry, but they seemed reluctant to talk. Every once in a while, someone leaving the caf would stop to ask the obvious question.

"Would you like some food?"

"If you want to."

Nearly all the haggard individuals camped outside the cafeteria were students in Professor Richard Leitch's First Term Seminar (FTS), "The Politics of Homelessness." For three nights and three days, beginning on Sunday evening, November 14, 2010, they adopted a life of simulated homelessness. They abandoned their dorm rooms, cell phones, laptops, and meal plans. They went to classes as usual and slept where they could—often outdoors. The idea was to make students aware of the daily struggles and indignities of being homeless. And the lessons seemed to sink in.

"I'm exhausted," said Jenni Harms '14. "I can understand now why homeless kids drop out or don't do well in school, because I can barely focus in class, and I've been homeless for only three days."

Leitch's homelessness class is among the most quickly-filled First Term Seminars at Gustavus. Its popularity reflects the **idealism** that many freshmen carry with them when they arrive on campus. Some students choose to act on their ideals by volunteering. Others become activists for a cause. The students in Leitch's FTS do not engage in activities that directly help the homeless, but they do gain the kind of empathy that can lead to good works.

"We realize that a true homeless person's experience is much more difficult than anything we will encounter," Leitch says, "but at least it gives us a better understanding what [that] reality must be like for homeless people."[1]

BELOW: *Students from Professor Richard Leitch's "Politics of Homelessness" seminar brave sub-freezing temperatures during the final night of their "sleep-out."*

During the College's early years, idealistic Gusties often channeled their efforts toward Christian missionary work, both at home and abroad.

In 2006, the Campus Activities Board began sponsoring a new fundraising event—Dancing with the Profs.

Volunteerism went global in 1962 when Jerry Springston, Kay Jurgenson, and Bruce Thorson became the first Gusties to join the Peace Corps.

Erin Luhmann '08 served for two years with the Peace Corps in Kyrgyzstan. In recent years, Gustavus has consistently ranked among the top small-college producers of Peace Corps volunteers.

The experience [in the Peace Corps] changed my life. I became a minister in no small part because of the influence of missionaries with whom I worked. I had studied Swedish at Gustavus, never imagining that I would use it working with missionaries from Sweden in Ethiopia!

- Jerry Springston '62

Gustavus students sod the yard of a Habitat for Humanity house in St. Peter, 2010.

Students from the "Changing the World" J-Term class organize a key chain sale to benefit victims of the 2010 Haitian earthquake.

I IDEALISM

Gustavus Republicans show their support for presidential candidate Wendell Wilkie in 1940. During most of its first century, Gustavus was known as a politically conservative campus.

Anti-war sentiment made its first appearance on campus in the years leading up to World War II.

By the mid-1960s, the civil rights movement and the anti-Vietnam war movement were beginning to make themselves felt on campus.

Pacifists at Gustavus will participate in an international student peace strike scheduled for one hour on Friday, April 12, from 11 a.m. to noon, as an expression of disapproval of militarism in all forms. • *Gustavian Weekly,* April 9, 1935

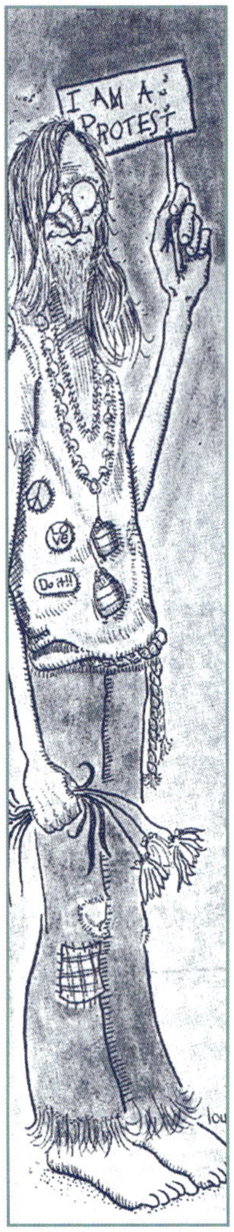

One of the first mass protests at Gustavus— an anti-war march in the spring of 1970.

A group of about 75 Gustavus students met closed doors when they attempted to present the Nicollet County Draft Board, located in St. Peter, with an indictment for murder. The presentation was part of the continuing protest against the war.
• *Gustavian Weekly,* April 17, 1970

The students, faculty, and administration of Gustavus Adolphus College . . . declare Wednesday, May 6, 1970, as a "Day of Involvement." In observance all members of the academic community are urged to participate in special programs and to turn class discussions to issues of the day. • **Gustavus news release following the Kent State shootings on May 4, 1970**[2]

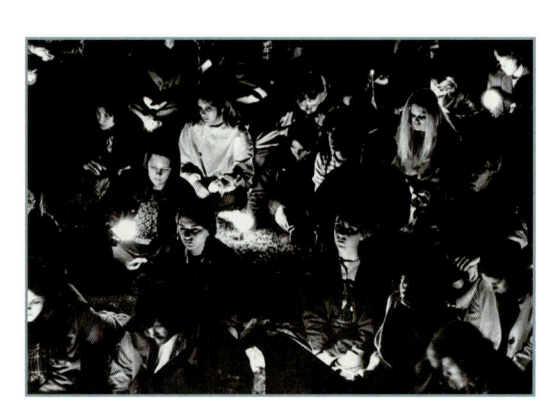

All-night "Sing-in for Peace" outside Christ Chapel, 1971

In the spring of 1970, students rallied to save a small grove of cedar trees slated for removal in preparation for construction of the new administration building. Although the student activists declared victory, President Frank Barth later claimed that his wife, Marge, was the person most responsible for saving the trees.[3]

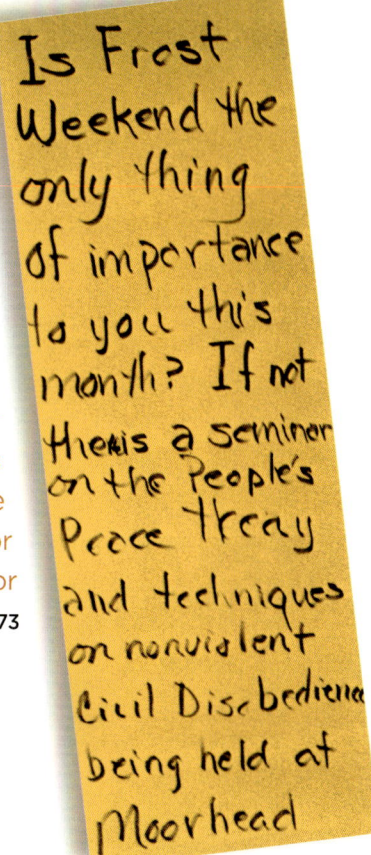

Campus activism largely dissipated in the years following the end of the Vietnam War.

> It seems doubtful that a real potential for mass student protest any longer exists at Gustavus. When the warm spring sun recharges our collegiate batteries and we start heading for our swimming holes and outdoor beer busts, let's pause a moment in remembrance of the Gustavus activist movement [of the late 1960s and early 1970s] . . . or maybe get together and throw a good old fashioned protest—just for old times' sake. • **None of the Above** (student newspaper), April 6, 1973

Is Frost Weekend the only thing of importance to you this month? If not there is a seminar on the People's Peace Treaty and techniques on nonviolent Civil Disobedience being held at Moorhead

"Tabling" for fair trade outside the Caf, 2009.

In recent decades, student activists have continued to express their views on issues they consider important. In 1989, when the College's trustees reconsidered their decision to divest in companies doing business in apartheid South Africa, students and faculty peacefully demonstrated outside Christ Chapel.

JOURNEY

Kareen Getfield '12 came a long way to attend Gustavus. Born in Jamaica, raised in New York City, she had come to campus for the first time in early 2008. Her visit coincided with the annual Building Bridges Conference featuring Rwandan genocide resister Paul Rusesabagina. It was then that she decided Gustavus was for her. "There was something about that moment that made me realize this was where I belonged," she said.[1]

Kareen knew that Gustavus offered no major in the subjects that interested her most—African and African American history—but she wasn't worried. She discovered early in her first year that the College's extensive study abroad programs would give her the chance to **journey** to almost any country she chose. In August 2010, after more than a year of preparation, she departed for her dream destination—the West African nation of Ghana.

For four months, Kareen attended classes at the University of Ghana. Her hosts—an extended family of parents, grandparents, uncles, aunts, and cousins—treated her as a daughter. "They were amazing," Kareen said. "They were genuine, down to earth. They immediately made me feel welcome."[2]

About a month into her stay, Kareen embarked on a field trip to Elmina Castle, one of the last architectural remnants of the Atlantic slave trade. "I didn't know how I would react," she later recalled. "Would I start crying? I wasn't sure."[3] In a journal entry a few days later, she described her time at the castle as "the most emotional, mental, and exhausting experience I have ever encountered."[4]

It took several months for Kareen to digest what she saw at Elmina, but by the time she returned to Gustavus, the lessons had crystallized. "Yes, they were captured," she said of the millions of slaves who passed through the castle, "but you can see how strong they were. They persevered. They endured. . . . Now I've had first-hand experience in seeing this. It's made me a stronger person to know that I can overcome and I can achieve anything. If they can do that, there's nothing I can't do."[5]

RIGHT: *Kareen Getfield '12 in the "Door of No Return," at Ghana's Elmina Castle, 2010.*

Sara Hansen '89 at Stonehenge, 1988

George Stevens, Department of Biology, in Costa Rica, 1986

Looking at something from another angle always gives one a new perspective, and seeing Gustavus, home and the States from the outside, so to speak, is no different. I'm beginning to see where my values lie and whether they should be adjusted or not. • Laurie Battey '82[6]

An incoming first-year student considers study abroad options, 2010.

The new curriculum [including the addition of Winter Term] has expanded the campus to world-wide dimensions. What would have been impossible a few years ago in terms of time and travel is almost commonplace to the Gustavus student of today . . . [Gustavus's] entire Intercultural Education program involved over 200 students on study tours throughout Europe, the continental United States, Puerto Rico, and Mexico.
• 1966 *Gustavian*

Kelly Nelson '10 in Shravanbelagola, India, 2008

21 Gustavus students and their faculty co-leaders were visiting Machu Picchu, Peru, when floodwaters cut off all roads in the area in late January 2010. The Gusties were stranded for four days while they waited for rescue crews to evacuate them.

JOURNEY

Thanks to a chance meeting between Coach George B. Myrum, Gustavus athletic director, and Filiberto Gomez, student of El Paso University of Mexico City, the Gustie basketball team will travel to the Mexican capital this spring and engage in the first international athletic tournament that a Gustavus team has ever participated in. ¶ And thanks to that same meeting, Mr. Gomez has enrolled as a junior at Gustavus, majoring in physical education. • *Gustavian Weekly,* February 15, 1938

Chinese sophomore Chin Hsuan Wang, shown here in 1929, was among the first non-Scandinavian international students to attend Gustavus.[7]

International students began attending Gustavus in larger numbers in the years immediately following World War II.
BELOW, LEFT TO RIGHT: *Erick Jensen, Denmark, 1947; John Magalee, British Guiana, 1947; Seifu Selassie, Ethiopia, 1948*

The students [at Gustavus] are so much more friendly than I had expected—and the professors! Everyone is so good. I will say that I like it here, and I am glad to be a Gustie. • Erick Jensen, Denmark, 1947[8]

Filiberto Gomez '39 of Mexico attended Gustavus at the urging of Coach George Myrum, who met him during the basketball team's 1938 trip to Mexico City.[9]

LEFT: *Jim Cho, Korea, and Niels Sorenson, Denmark, 1952;*
ABOVE: *Bim Davis, Sierra Leone, and Jyrki Tuukanan, Finland, 1954*

1954 Cosmopolitan Club

These scholars from other lands represent an integral part of the Gustavus family. With inquiring and tolerant minds they make possible a reciprocal relationship whereby we discover that just as we have many illusions about others, so are there many misconceptions about us. • 1956 *Gustavian*

I kinda like my foreign roommate. I mean, he's different—eats strange stuff, wears clothes I wouldn't, and has a name that's a little tricky to pronounce. But we get along just fine most of the time. He's been trying to teach me what they call football; we sometimes play it with his foreign friends. It's weird. • Henrick Nilsson, 1981[10]

Students from Kansai University in Japan enjoy lunch on the lawn outside Uhler Hall, 1975. The student and faculty exchange program with Kansai helped Gustavus correct an imbalance between west and east in the international studies program.[11]

Each year Gustavus's International Cultures Club sponsors an International Festival featuring student and faculty entertainment and displays.

The caf service is like living at a hotel for me. In my country almost all students live in their own apartment and have to buy groceries and cook by themselves. • Eva Klammeus, Sweden, 1989[12]

K KITCHENS

It promised to be, by Evelyn Young's own reckoning, the climax of a long, eventful, and successful career. King Carl XVI Gustaf of Sweden was coming to Gustavus Adolphus, and the College intended to give him the royal treatment—culminating in a banquet for 2,000 people in the recently completed Lund Arena. As director of the Gustavus food service, "Ma" Young (as she was affectionately known by nearly everyone on campus) took it upon herself to make sure that the meal went off without a hitch.

Planning had begun six months earlier. Evelyn spent weeks perfecting a menu featuring Cornish game hens a l'orange, Chippewa wild rice, and hot cross buns. She hired more than 125 student servers and supervised a series of dress rehearsals to make sure everyone involved knew where they needed to be, and when.

When the king finally sat down at his table, as scheduled, at 11:15 a.m. on April 9, 1976, "Ma" Young's crew went to work. "We got 2,000 people served in 19 minutes flat," she later boasted.

No one who knew Evelyn Young was surprised that she managed to stage a royal banquet with hardly a hiccup. She had been performing minor gastronomic miracles at Gustavus since 1949. The former Evelyn Sponberg was a Gustavus graduate (1933) and a former schoolteacher who had learned to cook for large groups while supervising the restaurant at a Northfield bowling alley that she and her husband, Gus, operated. When Gustavus hired Gus to be its new basketball coach in 1949, Evelyn assumed command of the College's **kitchens** and food service.

She quickly established herself as a beloved figure on campus—a hard-working and demanding dervish with a genuine fondness for the students she fed. She baked birthday cakes for students (for a small fee), packed bag lunches for picnics, and kept the price of a cup of coffee at five cents when almost every other diner and restaurant in the country was charging more. "We do things to make them feel that Gustavus is their home away from home," she said. "I know that's an old cliché, but it's true."[1]

BELOW, LEFT TO RIGHT: *Evelyn Young '33 (left) and bakers Anna Johnson and Lillian Hanson show off a few loaves of "Mom's rye bread," 1965.*

In 1992, the college called Evelyn out of retirement to be the public face of a new fundraising campaign.

An early food service photo probably taken inside the kitchen in Johnson Hall.

THE "HASH FACTORY" Many Gustavus students took their meals at off-campus boarding clubs in the years following the closing of the college's boarding department (better known as the "hash factory") in 1902.

The House of Seven Gables boarding club, 1904

> K
>
> Wednesday, we had beefsteak and herring, tomatoes and catsup for dinner. That is the height of extravagance.
>
> • • •
>
> **Student journal, 1890[2]**

Kemp's boarding club, 1904

In 1924, a cafeteria for all students opened in the basement of Old Main. Students continued to take their meals there until 1945.

> *We board at the students' table for $1.75 per week. . . . We have clear coffee for breakfast and dinner, and tea for supper with sugar and cream on the table to put in yourself, brown and white bread on the same plate, then they have potatoes, and some dish of vegetables with pudding for dessert or apples. . . . They keep three cows, and told us we can have plenty of milk to drink and I see they use it freely in the preparation of food.*

- Mrs. J.A. Bauman, faculty wife, on Gustavus food service, 1881[3]

The College Cafeteria SERVES FOOD
That you will like to eat at prices you are willing to pay.
"The best place to eat."

Most of the time it is simply taken for granted that, every day, mother presents for her eager boarders, three palatable meals, beside the little incidental snacks between times. Usually we are inclined to accept it all as a matter of course. However, there come times when we throw our arms around mother and tell her that, after all, no one else in the whole world can make apple pie quite so tasty as she does, or prepare that salad so fresh and crispy.

- *Gustavian Weekly,* March 5, 1925

$10.00 COUPON BOOK
Nº 6714
COLLEGE CAFETERIA
ST. PETER, MINN.
SOLD TO Ruth Tikner
NOT TRANSFERABLE
WE ARE NOT RESPONSIBLE FOR THE LOSS OF THIS BOOK
NATIONAL CHECKING COMPANY
ST. PAUL CHICAGO NEW YORK

KITCHENS

"LET US HELP YO'ALL (you all) START THE NEW YEAR OUT RIGHT"

For those special occasions make the Dining Room your eating headquarters during 1949.

Mr. Leonard Matson, Chef

The College Dining Room

In 1945, the cafeteria moved from Old Main to the lower level of the east wing of Uhler Hall. A dining room for "special occasions" was added in 1948.

Complaints about long cafeteria lines date back to the earliest days of the Gustavus food service.

I, for one, haven't too many complaints [about the Gustavus food service] because when I get hungry, anything tastes good to me—even shrimp wiggles.

- Beverly Bonn '53[4]

Students finally had some room to spread out when the new cafeteria in the new Student Union opened in 1960. An addition to the Student Union in 1966 added even more room.

THIS REMINDS ME OF G.A.C's NEW CAFETERIA POLICY.

NUMBER PLEASE—

Nowhere do you encounter a line such as [the one at the Gustavus cafeteria] unless perhaps you try to buy a pint of kerosene at a Russian Soviet store.

- *Gustavian Weekly,* September 25, 1934

This weekend . . . when our parents are here [for Parents' Weekend], the food will probably be quite good so that our parents will say, "I think this food is good. How can you kids complain so much?" A good answer to this question is to tell them to make a surprise visit for the Friday evening meal. • *Gustavian Weekly,* October 10, 1969

A Parents Weekend cry for help, 1965.

The new Market Place food court—established in 1999—featured station-to-station browsing and a multitude of choices. Its opening brought an end to the old Gustavus food service model—assembly line counter service combined with an all-you-can-eat policy. The Princeton Review has consistently ranked Gustavus's dining service among the top 20 in the nation.

> *With all the other pressures going on in the lives of our students, we don't want what they had for dinner to be the worst part of their day. In fact, maybe it should be the best part of their day.*
> • Steve Kjellgren '86, dining service director (1994–present)

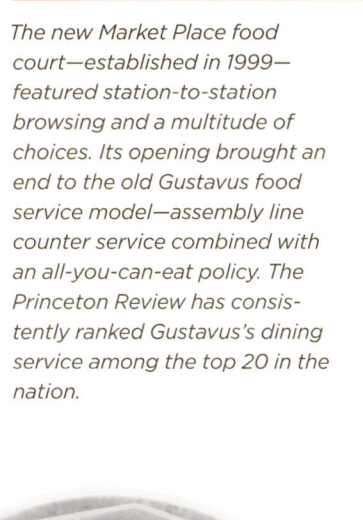

Renee Guittar '12 monitors the tomatoes' progress at Big Hill Farm. In 2009, the Gustavus Dining Service began incorporating fresh produce from the student-run organic farm, located on the edge of campus.

In an effort to reduce waste, the Dining Service introduced Gustieware, a reusable alternative to cardboard carryout containers, in 2008.

47

L LANDMARKS

The people of St. Peter had never witnessed anything like the celebration that took place in their town on Reformation Day, October 31, 1876. Horses and wagons clogged the streets. Trains pulled into the Omaha depot one by one, carrying passengers from the far-off cities of St. Paul, Minneapolis, and Red Wing. When everyone had arrived, the parade began. With band playing and banners waving, a long line of marchers made its way up the hill on the west side of town and finally came to a stop at the new building that had been erected on its crest. A choir sang. Dignitaries spoke (mostly in Swedish). The building, an imposing four-story edifice made of local Kasota stone, was officially dedicated "to God, the Church, and the Cause of Education."

The building on the hill represented a new commitment to higher learning among the Swedish immigrants of Minnesota. Fourteen years earlier, in 1862, a Swedish Lutheran clergyman named Eric Norelius had started a small school in Red Wing. The school then moved to the town of East Union, where it was known as St. Ansgar's Academy. Now, with the blessing of the Augustana Synod's Minnesota Conference, the school had moved again, to St. Peter, and reinvented itself under a new name—Gustavus Adolphus College.

In the years that followed, the Gustavus campus gradually expanded outward from that first building on the hill. By 1926, a half-century after its dedication, the venerable structure—now known as Old Main—was one of eight buildings on campus. By then, it had become the College's primary identifying symbol, its image reproduced on postcards, commemorative plates, and countless other collectibles. And it remains a symbol today—a landmark among campus **landmarks**.[1]

An early view of the building that would later be known as Old Main.

HELLO WALK

Then there is Hello Walk—a grey slab of cold, hard cement covered with rustling leaves in the fall, ice and snow during the winter blasts, and ribbons of paint spelling out the jeers of Initiation Week. Hello Walk is not only the base of a giant isosceles triangle; it is the basis upon which enduring friendships are laid, tradition is born and nurtured, and a college is formed.

• 1957 *Gustavian*

GUS

The noble bust in the mall, that of Gustavus Adolphus (commonly "Old Gus"), has also witnessed with an imperious eye many . . . night raids. He has worn watermelon and pumpkin helmets, been painted, muffled in scarves, worn beanies, smoked cigarettes, sucked pacifiers—in short, lived a well-rounded life. • *Gustavian Weekly,* October 15, 1965

GRANLUND SCULPTURES

Any time an artist dominates a scene as Paul did [at Gustavus], there's an impact that lives for generations beyond that artist's life. • Nicholas Legeros '77, sculptor[2]

LANDMARKS

WATER TOWER

In a flagrant display of disrespect to published decrees concerning the proper behavior of students on "Fraternity Initiation Night," one of the fraternities on the hill purposely and maliciously defaced the city water tower. It seems unthinkable that an organization which professes (whichever fraternity it should be) to adhere to college decisions should turn around and perform this most infamous infraction of acceptable behavior.

- *Gustavian Weekly,* April 28, 1950

The St. Peter water tower, located just north of Uhler Hall, was a frequent target of campus graffiti artists. The city removed the tower in 1984.

THE ROCK(S)

For more than a half century, Gusties have expended their creative energies on "The Rock"—usually with paint. But in one case, in 1966, a group of particularly ambitious pranksters actually replaced the rock with a smaller substitute.[3]

Although the exact origins of "The Rock," in front of Old Main, may forever be lost to history, it probably came from the field of small boulders that once dominated the landscape below campus.

THE SIGN

It may seem hard to believe, but the Gustavus Adolphus College sign at the top of College Avenue has not always been there. The sign, designed by Professor Don Gregory, first appeared in 1959, and was made possible by gifts from the classes of 1953 and 1958.[4]

THE ARB

The Arboretum got a big boost this year when people figured out that they could get a tan and plant trees at the same time. We can all come back fifty years from now and [lie] under the shade of our own little tan perpetrator.

• 1975 *Gustavian*

The Linnaeus Arboretum dates its genesis to 1972, when President Frank Barth expressed a desire to have "a few trees" planted around the new president's residence on the western edge of the campus. The college botanist, Charles Mason, responded with a plan to create an arboretum on adjacent college-owned farmland.[5]

THE SPIRE

It all comes back to that beam of light coming from and, I still believe, to the chapel spire. I now notice it every time I look toward the chapel at night. No matter where I am, as long as I can see or am close to the chapel, the light finds me. • Steve Ellwein '98[6]

MORTARBOARDS

The first graduates of Gustavus Adolphus College—the Class of 1890—were, in the words of President Matthias Wahlstrom, "eight young men who would blaze the way." Wahlstrom had struggled for the better part of a decade to transform Gustavus from a college preparatory academy into a true, degree-granting institution of higher learning. Powerful voices among Minnesota's Swedish American Lutherans had questioned the need for a new college, but Wahlstrom prevailed. The commencement exercises on May 15, 1890, constituted a sweet victory. "The struggle was won!" Wahlstrom proclaimed.[1]

Among the highlights of that first commencement was a speech delivered by one of the eight graduates—Lars P. Lundgren. Like many of the commencement speakers who followed him in years to come, Lundgren spoke of the future. But he took the exercise one step beyond the expected: he imagined what Gustavus would look like a half century later. His predictions included:

"Splendid buildings of learning, which in size and splendor can be compared with any such buildings in America."

A library, with "many thousands of volumes."

A music hall housing a "musical department . . . second to none in America."

A gymnasium where "boys and girls [grow] strong and limber."

And finally, a chapel, "whose pleasant spire . . . points upward to Him, who is the school's helper and protector."

Most of Lundgren's predictions came true, although some took longer than 50 years to reach fruition. The optimism he expressed set an example that scores of commencement speakers, decked out in black robes and **mortarboards**, later echoed. Even today, his closing words strike a familiar chord.

"The young people that found and shall find inexhaustible treasures here, shall exhort their friends to come, seek, and find what they need for a happy life. And [their] parents . . . shall not only send them here, but build houses in which their children can live, study, and be happy."[2]

BELOW: *Class of 1890 with Lars Lundgren standing, far left.*

The graduating Class of 1900 processes down College Hill for commencement exercises at First Lutheran Church.

For several years, up to 1920, seniors gathered for a pre-graduation breakfast on top of Old Main. Eventually, perhaps because of safety concerns, the breakfast was moved to the lawn below.

The male, female, short, tall, and in between members of the Class of 1908.

> Hardest thought of all is leaving friends—those old, and those recently acquired. The shoulder you were wont to weep on will soon be some 500 miles away. The pal who helped you waste your time in such delightful fashion will soon be placed in that vague but inevitable pigeon-hole called memory.
> • Bob Redeen '39[3]

The Class of 1924.

MORTARBOARDS

CONGRATULATIONS '57ers FROM Faust DRUGS
Your Headquarters For The Best In
COSMETICS
PRESCRIPTIONS
STATIONERY   TOBACCO
"The Friendly Store"

Scenes from Commencement 1957.

Commencement 1968—Lie Aan Tan of Indonesia receives his diploma from President Edgar Carlson.

We are born into chaos
And suckled by the infinite miseries of erupting bones
*   and muddled minds.*
Socrates and Liebnitz and Wordsworth are tiny needles
*   pointed at the base of the brain, and yet*
There is more order in the hyacinth
And more knowledge in the smell of wet grass on some
*   green forgotten morning.*
We have either grown old
Or wise.

- Bill Holm '65[4]

What a difference a decade makes. Commencement exercises in 1961 (below) and 1971 (right)

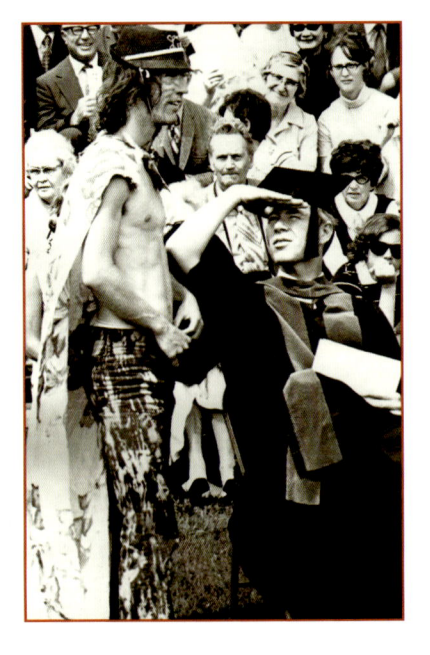

A most interesting occurrence happened at commencement in the spring of 1971. I was shaking the hands of graduating seniors when one of them handed me a live duck as I reached to shake his hand. I tucked the duck under my left arm and continued shaking hands until a young fellow I knew was willing to take the duck from me.

- Frank Barth, president, 1969–75[5]

Gradually you realize you are just one cookie in another batch of Gusties coming out of the oven and ready to be examined under the cookie counter of life. • **1976**
Gustavian

Commencement 1976

Commencement 2008

*For those of us who walk behind,
You graduates are an answer to the question,
    what is the difference?
You embody the days of our years.
You take with you a part of our lives we have lived in
For a visionary moment; you are an ancient procession
    of pilgrims
Passing through a holy wayside,
A symbol of our human aspiration,
A symbol of divine grace.*

• Richard Elvee, chaplain[6]

GUSTAVUS ADOLPHUS COLLEGE TIMELINE

1862 Eric Norelius establishes "school for Swedes" in Red Wing

1863 School relocates to church in East Union under principal Andrew Jackson (1863–73)

Norelius

1865 School renamed St. Ansgar's Academy

1866 St. Ansgar's moves to nearby property donated by Scandinavian veterans of the Civil War

Jackson

1873 John Frodeen (1873–74) succeeds Jackson as principal

1874 Andrew Jackson (1874–76) returns as acting principal

Frodeen

1876 School renamed Gustavus Adolphus College; relocates to new building (later known as Old Main) in St. Peter under President Jonas Nyquist (1876–81)

1881 Matthias Wahlstrom (1881–1904) assumes presidency

Nyquist

1884 North Hall, South Hall, and president's residence (later known as the White House) completed

Wahlstrom

1886 Gymnasium completed

1887 Commerce Building completed

1890 First college class graduates

1902 Chartered train carries about 250 Gustavus students to inaugural state oratorical contest in Northfield; first intercollegiate football game (Gustavus 11, Mankato Normal 6)

1903 Minnesota Conference of Augustana Synod tables proposal to move Gustavus to the Twin Cities

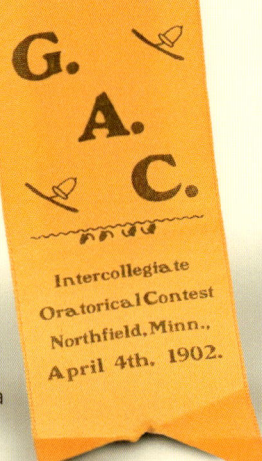

Independent Blessings, circa 1911

1904 Peter Mattson (1904–11) assumes presidency; Auditorium completed; the first sorority precursors, the "Independent Blessings" and "TMT" (limited-membership literary societies), are established

Mattson

"Old Main" at G.A.C.

56

1862–1946

1905 All intercollegiate sports banned at Gustavus

1906 The first fraternity precursors, the "Olympian Council" (limited-membership debating society) and the "Reds" (secret society) are established

1910 All intercollegiate sports except football reinstated at Gustavus; Johnson Hall completed

1911 Jacob Uhler (1911–13) assumes acting presidency

1913 O. J. Johnson (1913–42) assumes presidency

1917 Intercollegiate football reinstated at Gustavus

1920 Two secret societies, the "Reds" and the "Grays," are officially recognized as legitimate limited membership societies

Johnson

the Grays

1922 New Gymnasium (later known as O.J. Johnson Student Union) completed

The "Heavies" vs. the "Leans"

1923 Women's football game between the "Heavies" and the "Leans" makes national headlines

1929 Stadium and Uhler Hall completed; first in a series of international debates between Gustavus and British universities including Oxford and Cambridge; first night football game in Minnesota held at Gustavus's new stadium

1932 Unveiling of the bust of King Gustavus Adolphus

1938 Coach George Myrum and two students killed in bus crash; Rundstrom Hall completed

1939 Myrum Memorial Fieldhouse completed

1941 MIAC suspends Gustavus from conference play for one year

1942 Walter Lunden (1942–43) assumes presidency

1943 Navy V-12 training unit established; O. A. Winfield (1943–44) assumes acting presidency

Lunden

Carlson

1944 Edgar Carlson (1944–68) assumes presidency

1946 Ranch House completed

GUSTAVUS ADOLPHUS COLLEGE TIMELINE

1947 Classroom Annex completed

1948 Bernadotte Library and Wahlstrom Hall completed

1949 Art Barn completed

1950 Folke Bernadotte Memorial Foundation established

1951 Inga Carlson competes as diver on Gustavus men's swimming team, prompting MIAC ban on women on men's teams

1955 Sorensen Hall completed

1960 Food Service Building and Heating Plant completed; first graduating class of Gustavus's nursing program

1961 Christ Chapel, Edwin J. Vickner Hall of Language Arts, and Sohre Hall completed

1963 26 Nobel laureates participate in dedication of Alfred Nobel Hall of Science; Valley View Hall (later known as Pittman Hall) completed; new curriculum, including 4-1-4 academic calendar, introduced; Gustavus sponsors competition in women's gymnastics—first intercollegiate competition for women in more than 50 years

1965 First Nobel Conference: "Genetics and the Future of Man"

1966 Link (later known as Gibbs Hall) completed

1967 Co-ed (later known as Norelius Hall) completed

1968 Albert Swanson (1968–69) assumes acting presidency

1969 Frank Barth (1969–75) assumes presidency

1970 Fire destroys Auditorium

1971 Schaefer Fine Arts Center and President's House completed

Barth

1972 Edgar M. Carlson Administration Building and Folke Bernadotte Memorial Library completed

1973 A.H. Anderson Social Science Center completed; inaugural presentation of Christmas in Christ Chapel; Jill Lindquist '74 joins men's soccer team, becomes first recognized female player in MIAC history

1975 Edward A. Lindell (1975–80) assumes presidency; Lund Arena completed

1977 Gustavus Library Associates established

Lindell

1978 Gustavus Athletics Hall of Fame established with 19 charter members

1979 Gustavus Adolphus College Arboretum (later Linnaeus Arboretum) dedicated

1980 Abner W. Arthur (1980–81) assumes acting presidency; first men's national team championship: men's tennis

1981 John S. Kendall (1981–91) assumes presidency

1982 First women's national title: gymnastics

Kendall

1947–2012

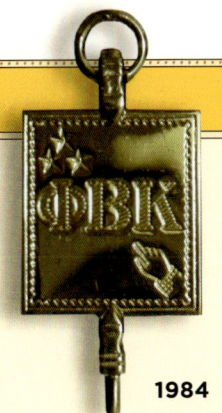

1983 Gustavus granted Phi Beta Kappa charter

1984 Lund Center completed

1988 College View Apartments and Melva Lind Interpretive Center completed

1989 Curriculum II introduced

1991 Axel Steuer (1991–2002) assumes presidency; F.W. Olin Hall and Ogden P. Confer Hall completed

1992 Swanson Tennis Center completed

1998 Tornado devastates campus; Prairie View Hall completed; Arbor View Apartments purchased

2000 C. Charles Jackson Campus Center and Carlson International Center completed

Steuer

2002 Dennis J. Johnson named president (2002–03)

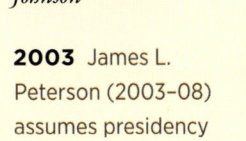

Johnson

2003 James L. Peterson (2003–08) assumes presidency

Peterson

2005 Southwest Hall completed

2007 Hollingsworth Field and Stadium completed

2008 Jack R. Ohle assumes presidency

2009 College's brand "Make Your Life Count" established

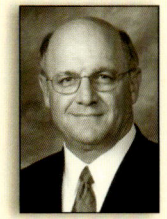

2010 Center for Servant Leadership established

Ohle

2011 New Academic Building completed and named in honor of Warren Beck '67 and Donna Gabbert Beck '66

Gusties Will Shine!

NOTABLES

The editors of Gustavus's 1909 yearbook, *Valkyria*, wanted to do something that would make their publication stand out from the College's two previous annuals, which had been published in 1904 and 1906. The solution they devised proved to be an ingenious one, and it helped mold the College's image over the next quarter century. Not only that, it introduced to campus one of its first true **notables**—a personality who touched the lives of countless students and left behind a unique body of work.

His name was Eben E. Lawson.

Lawson was the cartoonist for the *Willmar Tribune*. In 1909, the juniors responsible for the publication of *Valkyria* hired Lawson to draw cartoons of each member of the college's junior and senior classes. The results were stunning. Lawson's skill as a caricaturist was undeniable, but what made his work truly stand out was the preparation he put into each drawing. Lawson reveled in the company of students. He spent hours upon hours at St. Peter's Ideal Café, talking with groups of Gusties, figuring out who they were, distilling their essence. One of his many student friends claimed that, "in a sporadic, checkered, coffee-loving, cigar-reeking career of little sleep and much talk at Gustavus, Mr. Lawson heard more confidences and secrets—and kept them—than any other person."

Lawson returned to Gustavus at irregular intervals over the years that followed, capturing the personalities, accomplishments, and foibles of scores of Gustavus students. Most of his cartoons included a pair of ducks—"Gus" and "Adolph"—who commented on the action going on around them. Gus and Adolph were, in the words of a writer for the *Gustavus Quarterly*, "as prominent in the memories of many Gustavians as the bronze bust of Gustavus or Old Main itself."

Eben Lawson continued to draw for Gustavus yearbooks until 1931. He died twenty years later in his hometown of Willmar. He was, wrote a former student, "one of the best friends the school ever had."[1]

BELOW, LEFT TO RIGHT: *Eben Lawson, 1931*
Evelyn Wingstrand, 1922
Franz Benjamin Andreen, 1917
College seal, 1909

HALLANDER: CAMPUS CUSTODIAN

As a respected old gentleman and a confidential friend Mr. [Ernest] Hallander has found a rare place in the hearts of the students of this college . . . Hallander delights to chat with his young and firm friends and on many occasions when his few spare moments chance around you will find him down in the furnace room, perhaps, with his circle of admiring boys seated on shovels or any other convenient support and eagerly drinking in his tales and witty sayings. They seek out his jolly company but duty calls him continually. • 1920 *Gustavian*

EMIL: CAMPUS CANINE

Years ago, in the misty past of Gustavus, a sprightly pup ambled leisurely up College Hill from some unknown hovel. His lineage was completely a mystery and so it has remained throughout his long and successful reign over the Gustavus campus. As the school years flew swiftly by, Emil grew to maturity in the scholarly atmosphere of college life. Graduating class after class filed from Gustavus's musty halls, but Emil remained on, continually storing up knowledge and wisdom which surpasses all human conception. • 1937 *Gustavian*

BARNEY: CAMPUS COP

If [colleague Harley Jordan and I] let a lot of things bother us, we'd go nuts. I just wish sometimes kids would think if they would want their fathers called some of them four letter words we get called once in a while. • Barney Lanham, 1971[2]

WILLIE: EQUIPMENT MANAGER

Willie [Lindquist] takes care of more than just the equipment. He's the father figure for most of the male athletes. He can build the players up or put them back in their place, depending on what they need. • Denny Raarup '53, retired football coach, 1988

NOTABLES

GOVERNORS In 1947, Gustavus historian Conrad Peterson wrote that the college "has specialized a bit in governors." At the time, Gustavus counted three Minnesota governors among its alumni. It added a fourth 20 years later.[3]

Adolph Eberhart 1895

Minnesota Governor John Lind (1899–1901) attended Gustavus's precursor institution, St. Ansgar's Academy, in 1869.

Minnesota Governor Adolph Eberhart (1909–15)

Luther Youngdahl 1919

Harold Levander '32

Minnesota Governor Luther Youngdahl (1947–51)

Minnesota Governor Harold Levander (1967–71)

Guess that Gustie!

Test your Gustavus IQ by matching each yearbook photo with its corresponding name and accomplishment.

- Internationally renowned expert on terrorism and counter-terrorism
- Storyteller and essayist
- First ALC woman pastor
- Television actor (*Six Feet Under*; *Parenthood*)
- Former president and CEO of Weight Watchers International
- Grammy-winning jazz vocalist

- Kurt Elling '89
- Barbara Andrews '58
- Bill Holm '65
- Allison Rosati '85
- Peter Krause '87
- Ruth Youngdahl Nelson '24
- Patsy O'Connell Sherman '52
- James McPherson '58
- Kevin Kling '79
- Linda Gulder Huett '66
- Clarence R. Magney 1903
- Magnus Ranstorp '85

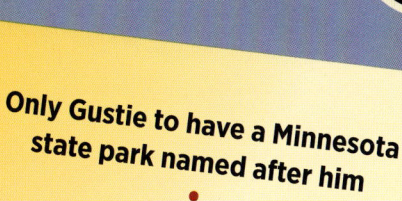

- Only Gustie to have a Minnesota state park named after him
- Poet and essayist
- News anchor, WMAQ-TV, Chicago
- 3M chemist and co-inventor of Scotchguard®
- 1973 National Mother of the Year
- Pulitzer Prize-winning author of *Battle Cry of Freedom*

(answers on pages 122–23)

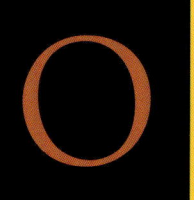

OCCASIONS

Five sophomore women space themselves evenly around an arrangement of poinsettias and evergreen cuttings in the narthex of Christ Chapel. Each holds an unlit candle. Each closes her eyes. With a long, flickering lighter in hand, Chaplain Rachel Larson circles the group, briefly pausing before each woman. After making a full circuit, she comes to a full stop and touches her flame to one of the candles. It takes a moment for the young woman who is holding it, Lainey Mikel '13, to realize she has just been chosen the 2010 St. Lucia. "I could feel it and see it, even though my eyes were closed," she admits. "It was a really beautiful reality. And symbolic as well."[1]

Few, if any, Gustavus **occasions** are as symbolic or enduring as the crowning of St. Lucia. Legend has it that many years ago, a maiden "clothed in white and crowned with light"—the martyred St. Lucia of Syracuse—brought food to Sweden during a great famine. The Swedes adopted Lucia as a symbol of hope and light, and celebrated her mythical appearance every December. In 1941 Gustavus held its first St. Lucia celebration.

As it happened, that initial festival of lights took place during one of the darkest moments in U.S. history—the days following the attack on Pearl Harbor.

Lainey Mikel is the 70th in a long line of St. Lucias. Like her predecessors, she was chosen for displaying qualities such as leadership, service, charity, and kindness. In the morning she will don a crown of candles and join the four members of her court on an excursion through the dormitories, singing Christmas carols to bleary-eyed classmates. She will read scripture at a special chapel service and attend a Scandinavian smörgåsbord luncheon.

And she will look the part.

Like most of the St. Lucias before her, Lainey is blonde. Light colored hair is not a prerequisite for St. Lucia candidates, but for many years tradition dictated otherwise. "St. Lucia . . . must have all the usual qualifications of a queen plus blonde hair," the *Gustavian Weekly* explained in 1951. "Red heads, brunettes, and even dishwater brownettes are excluded."[2]

LEFT TO RIGHT: *Lainey Mikel '13, shortly after her selection as the 2010 St. Lucia; Joan Onkka '52, 1949 St. Lucia; Naomi Hokanson '81, 1978 St. Lucia*

FAR LEFT: *Program for the 1959 Service of Nine Lessons and Carols. The annual worship service, which began in the mid 1950s, was the precursor of Christmas in Christ Chapel.*

LEFT: *Program for the 1988 presentation of Christmas in Christ Chapel, a holiday tradition that began in 1973.*

> Christmas is always a nice time of year at Gustavus. People change from final-pending monsters to secret Santas in one day. You can go to Christmas in Christ Chapel and see people who've never set foot inside of the chapel in four years.
>
> • 1975 *Gustavian*

1975

2008

For more than three decades, Gustavus Library Associates' biennial "A Royal Affair" gala benefit has served as the primary fundraiser for the College's Folke Bernadotte Memorial Library.

OCCASIONS

HOMECOMING Gustavus held its first homecoming in 1922 during the basketball season. The first football season homecoming took place in 1926. The college chose its first homecoming queen in 1935 and continued to do so until 1971, when the student body elected to abandon the tradition. The tradition was revived in 1986 with the coronation of a homecoming queen *and* king.

The Delta Phi Omega sorority's classic "Flush the Johnnies" 1970 homecoming float.

The Tau Psi Omega fraternity bargain basement entry in the 1974 homecoming parade.

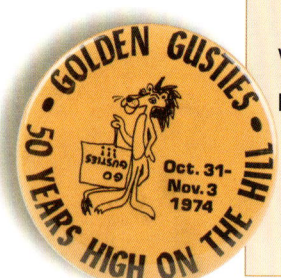

> "50 Years High on the Hill" was the Homecoming theme this year. What do you suppose that meant?
>
> • • •
>
> 1975
> *Gustavian*

The coronation of a homecoming king and queen is a tradition that is being brought back to Gustavus after a 15-year absence. By having campus organizations nominate people, [student activities adviser Machell] Kvanli says, "We're trying to make it not just a popularity contest." • *Gustavian Weekly,* October 9, 1986

1949 homecoming queen candidates

2009 homecoming royalty, Matt Schueffner '10 and Alex Brakke '10

FROST Frost Weekend, a midwinter tradition, got its start at Gustavus in 1949. It continued until 1983, when concerns about alcohol abuse led to its cancellation.

1962 Frost Queen Jaynice Hafdahl '63

Frost Weekend broomball, 1970s

Everyone told me I had fun [during Frost Weekend], but I really can't remember it. • **Gustavus senior, 1974**[3]

MAY DAY Gustavus has long treated the first week of May as a special time on the calendar. For many years it was a time for spring concerts and May Day festivals—complete with the coronation of a May queen. In recent years, it has become a time for recognizing student achievement (Honors Day) and exploring issues of peace and disarmament (the annual MAYDAY! Conference).

Honors Day procession, 2010

Students in Swedish costume dance around a maypole during the 1951 May Day celebration.

2010 MAYDAY! Poster

PERFORMANCE

The Gustavus Adolphus Symphony Band was riding a wave of unprecedented, positive publicity when it set out, by bus, for the town of Cambridge, Minnesota, on March 16, 1941. Over the previous twelve days, the band had toured the state, making concert appearances in communities as far flung as Willmar, Minneapolis, and Duluth. Reviews were glowing and audiences were ecstatic. The band's student musicians reveled in the experience, as did the special guest who accompanied them, the internationally acclaimed composer and pianist Percy Grainger.

Grainger had spent two days at Gustavus the previous year, lecturing, conducting, and performing. He enjoyed his stay so much that he agreed to join the band on its 1941 tour.

Students savored the opportunity to perform with a world-renowned musician and Grainger was, in turn, impressed with the level of musical talent at Gustavus. "[The band] has perfect balance," he said. "And above all, it plays 'melody' instead of only rhythm as so many bands do, to the detriment of real symphonic development."

On March 16, the band embarked for Cambridge to give the final **performance** of its 1941 tour. But on the way, a late winter storm hit central Minnesota. Somewhere between Minneapolis and Cambridge, the bus stalled. The concert in Cambridge was in jeopardy. And then, to the amazement and delight of the band members and their director, Frederic Hilary, 5-foot-4-inch Percy Grainger jumped to the rescue. "He got out in his white duck pants, without coat or hat in the high wind, and pushed on the stalled bus," the *Gustavian Weekly* reported. Needless to say, the bus didn't budge, but for years after, many band members still smiled at the memory of the "bushy-haired, elfin pianist-composer" trying to push the band to Cambridge.

The concert in Cambridge was postponed until the next day. An alumnus who attended the performance insisted it was worth the wait. "I was never so proud of Gustavus as I am tonight," he said.[1]

BELOW: *An underdressed Percy Grainger on tour with the Gustavus Adolphus Symphony Band, 1941.*

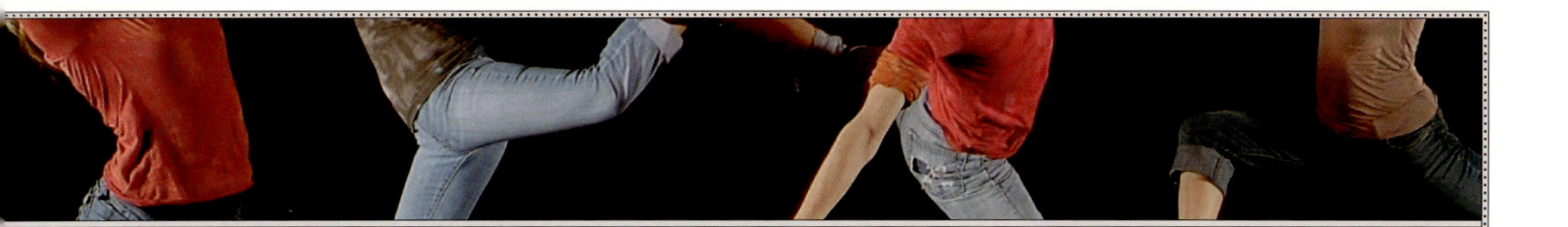

TOURING Many Gustavus musical groups have toured over the years—both domestically and internationally.

Gustavus Symphony Orchestra in China, 2008.

Pianist Ella Peterson won this medal for her performance in an 1894 campus music competition.

Instrumental and vocal soloists receive the audience's applause at the 2009 Honors Day recitals.

The Schumann women's chorus and Lyric men's chorus embark on their 1919 tour.

— P —

A liberal arts college is supposed to be a place of culture. And even though we are not required to distinguish Picasso's blue period from his black period, or to interpret Beethoven's Fifth before the sheepskin can be ours, we, as Gustavus graduates, will be expected by the world in general to have at least an acquaintance with the fine arts.

Gustavian Weekly,
May 15, 1959

Performance

MUSIC Over the years, Gustavus's music ensembles have played under a variety of names that today include Gustavus Wind Orchestra, Vasa Wind Orchestra, Gustavus Choir, Choir of Christ Chapel, Lucia Singers, St. Ansgar's Chorus, Birgitta Singers, Chamber Singers, Gustavus Philharmonic Orchestra, Gustavus Symphony Orchestra, Gustavus Jazz Lab Band, and Adolphus Jazz Ensemble. But no matter their names, they have consistently been known for the high quality of their musicianship.

2009

1904

BAND [The band's] instrumentalists are individualistic people; music majors are in the minority. It constitutes a pretty good cross-section of the student body. Where else, after all, can majors in philosophy and physical education sit peaceably side-by-side blowing their horns? • *None of the Above* (student newspaper), **November 10, 1972**

CHOIR It is a fine feeling to know that these canteen-going, P.O.-checking, book-cracking [singers of the Gustavus choir] each have a little bit of God in them, for [as the poet Johann Seume once wrote] "evil people have no song." • *Gustavian Weekly,* **February 21, 1969**

1961

2009

1907

ORCHESTRA Plans are moving along this year for the redevelopment of an orchestra and related string activities at Gustavus . . . Orchestral activities are not new to the campus although it is understood that strings have never been particularly strong. In recent years the almost total lack of string players has led to the abandonment of orchestral activities. • *Gustavus Quarterly,* **December 1964**

2009

THEATRE Fat Jack Falstaff, that loveable roguish tub of guts, wallows and rolls and flounders across the Gustavus stage this week. In his enormous wake are wives, fairies, fools, husbands, blackguards, panders, and sundry other folk. Go see them and join in the fun!
• *Gustavian Weekly,* October 30, 1964

Godspell, *1980*

The Merry Wives of Windsor, *1964*

The Glass Menagerie, *1997*

DANCE "Tell them about our zingy bodies."
"Ask 'em if they want a good laugh."
"Don't forget to say it's free with I.D."
"Let 'em know how much we've sweated and toiled."
"Okay, okay," I said to my fellow modern dance students and instructor Cindy Anderson. "I'll see if I can get that all in [an article]. That ought to get them to the concert. Now, should I put in the part about the skinny thighs?
• *Gustavian Weekly,* December 5, 1975

2009

OPERA Gustavus students who may perhaps feel a certain stigma attached to the opera, which kept them from viewing the performance, missed an evening (or afternoon, as the case may be) of unqualifiedly delightful entertainment. • *Gustavian Weekly,* May 10, 1957

The Impresario, *1956*

Q QUARTERS

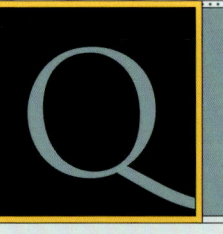

In the months following the end of World War II, administrators at Gustavus began making plans for what they assumed would be a major upheaval. Under the new G.I. Bill, the federal government pledged to provide college or vocational education to returning military veterans. Presumably some of those veterans would choose to attend Gustavus, but the college's administrators had no idea how many. At first they guessed the "G.I. bulge" would bump total enrollment to 700. In the spring of 1946, they revised their estimate upward, to 800—then 850. As the 1946-47 school year approached, applications for enrollment continued to inundate the admissions office. When the final numbers were tallied, they showed that enrollment at Gustavus had ballooned to 1,127, an all-time high.

The big question: where to put all those new students?

This was where all that post-war planning paid off. By the time classes began in September 1946, Gustavus was blossoming with new housing options. They weren't pretty, but they did the job they were supposed to do: they made it possible for several hundred students to attend Gustavus who might otherwise have been unable to do so.

About 100 of the new students, nearly all of them veterans, were housed in a new barracks-like building called the "ranch house," just west of Uhler Hall. Another 60 or so found temporary **quarters** in the basement of the Armory in downtown St. Peter. But the most visible new housing facilities were located in the parking lot adjacent to the Myrum Fieldhouse and the open field next to the football stadium. There, dozens of married couples—many of them with young children—set up house, either in government surplus trailer homes or in pre-fabricated houses. The trailers and "pre-fabs" provided only the most basic comforts, but most couples seemed grateful to have them. "Life was not easy," remembered one G.I. wife, "but most of us believed we'd look back and treasure the memories."[1]

LEFT: *The good life in Gustavus's "Trailer Town," 1946.*

From 1876 to 1884, on-campus housing was available only in Old Main, and it was reserved for male students.

In 1884, female students finally got their own dormitories when the College built two nearly identical buildings—South Hall (left) and North Hall—on either side of Old Main.

Every student in those days [of the late 1890s] was asked to bring a mattress, a pillow and some quilts. . . . The bedsteads had no springs, only a few slats. Toward the end of the term the straw [in our mattresses] had pulverized so that it settled in layers between the slats. The boys were sleeping more on slats than on straw. • J. L. Bergstrand 1902[2]

Student roomers at the Holteus house in St. Peter, about 1905.

Rising enrollment forced the College to add three new dormitories in the years before World War II: Johnson Hall (1910, far left), Uhler Hall (1929, left), and Rundstrom Hall (1938).

Living in the stadium prepared us for what was soon to follow, as most of us ended up in military service in World War II. Military life was a lark following life in the stadium. • Bob Hanson '42[3]

Continuing room shortages during the late 1930s forced the College to convert the athletic stadium's handball courts into student housing

QUARTERS

1938

1900

If you haven't lived in a dormitory, you really have missed something in college life. Noisy as they may be at times, the experiences and acquaintances encountered will remain among your memories forever. • **1941** *Gustavian*

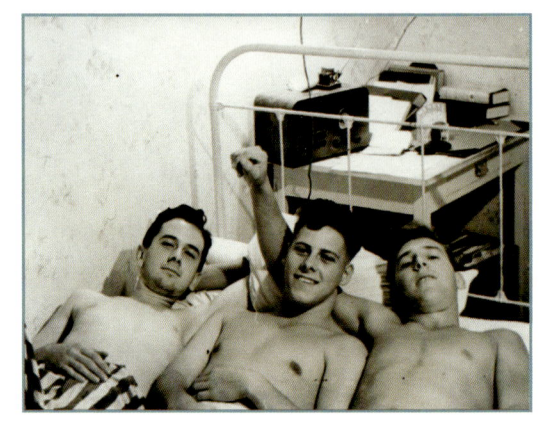

1941

You say you brought a 37-pound mounted moose head 500 miles to your new college dorm room and found out you can't hang it because it's against the rules to put nails in the plaster? . . . Don't crawl the walls looking for a solution. Poster art is the answer. Whether you want to cover a door or fill a space the size of a sheet of typewriter paper, a colorful, easy-to-hang poster reflecting almost any mood can be found. • *Gustavian Weekly,* October 3, 1980

1951

1908

2009

1904

A typical girl's room consists of at least one Solo Flex poster, a couple of photo albums, graduation pictures, high school yearbooks, a refrigerator stocked with Diet Coke, and almost always some baked goods from mom.
- *Gustavian Weekly,* October 15, 1987

A typical guy's room, on the other hand, never has food in the room (they go to the girl's room for that), and their refrigerator is stocked with beer. This goes well with the theme of the room, because covering the walls are beer posters and, let us not forget, the ever-popular beer light.
- *Gustavian Weekly,* October 15, 1987

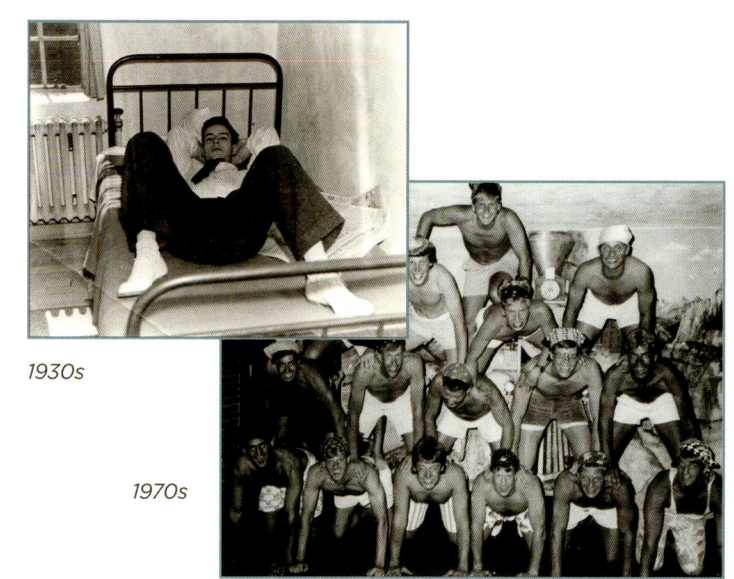

1930s

1970s

1973

Late night coeducational studying, 1967. During its first years of operation, the new Co-ed (later Norelius) Hall—with its notorious "Iron Curtain"— was truly coeducational only until 11 p.m.

REAL CO-ED LIVING IN CO-ED? INTERESTED? MEET IN SUM. I 7:30 3/23/71

After years of agitation from students, Gustavus began phasing in round-the-clock co-ed dormitory living in the early 1970s.

R RESILIENCE

The tornado that struck the Gustavus campus at 5:30 p.m. on Sunday, March 29, 1998, approached from the southwest. It was so wide (more than a mile across) and so low to the ground that it was hard to tell what it was. It looked more like a mass of blowing dust than a funnel cloud.

The twister hit the Linnaeus Arboretum first. Then it swept across the campus proper. Windows exploded. Roofs peeled away. Hundreds of trees—elms, cottonwoods, box elders, crabapples—toppled. Christ Chapel's spire snapped in half and crumpled onto the roof. (In contrast, the chapel's sanctuary lamp—the symbol of God's eternal presence—survived intact and continued to burn.)

And then it was over.

Hardly anyone was on campus when the storm hit. It was spring break. No one from the College community was killed or injured. But as news of the disaster spread, current and former Gustavians returned to campus to witness the destruction and help with the recovery.

"I remember standing at the base [of the hill], with my hand over my mouth," sociology major Angie Agan recalled. "The grass was supposed to be green, but the ground was brown with tree trunks and branches."

The tornado wreaked $50 million worth of devastation on Gustavus. Every building on campus suffered at least some damage. But in the days, weeks, and months that followed, the College demonstrated its **resilience**. The cleanup began almost immediately. Classes resumed after a three-week hiatus. Buildings were repaired. Trees were planted.

Six months after the storm, the College opened its 1998–99 academic year with a record enrollment of 2,474. "We have the newest roofs, trees, carpets and playing fields of any college in the country," President Alex Steuer told students at the opening chapel service. "We just wish the refurbishing could have been done in a less dramatic form."[1]

BOTTOM: *The finial atop Old Main was among the many architectural casualties of the tornado.*

"It's just part of the grieving process to come here and be with your classmates at a time like this. It's also important to me to see that, yes, Gustavus will be scarred. But it will come back.

• Tim Strand '82,
clean-up volunteer[2]

GUSTAVUS ADOLPHUS COLLEGE

AUTHORIZED CLEAN-UP CREW

As I look back, one of the important framing experiences of that disaster was that it happened during Holy Week. The events of death and resurrection were naturally surrounding us in the cycle of the church year. On Good Friday we sang a hymn. The first line was, "Tree of life and awesome mystery, in your death we are reborn." • Brian Johnson, chaplain, 2008[3]

The spire cross, which had been damaged in the 1998 tornado, returns to Christ Chapel for a special service marking the 10-year anniversary of the disaster.

R | RESILIENCE

THE CRASH The Gustavus community was forced to cope with one of the first true tragedies in its history when, on the morning of November 11, 1938, a bus carrying the Gustavus football team crashed on the way back to campus. Coach George Myrum and and students Donald V. Anderson '40 and Carl Olson '41 were killed.[4]

The accident occurred around 4:00 a.m., just north of Belle Plaine. The bus rear-ended a truck and crumpled in on itself.

Donald V. Anderson '40

Carl Olson '41

Coach George Myrum

The college's new Myrum Memorial Fieldhouse was completed four months after the accident.

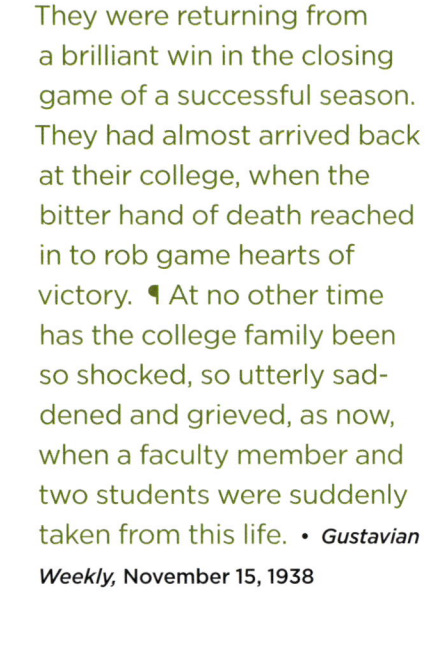

> They were returning from a brilliant win in the closing game of a successful season. They had almost arrived back at their college, when the bitter hand of death reached in to rob game hearts of victory. ¶ At no other time has the college family been so shocked, so utterly saddened and grieved, as now, when a faculty member and two students were suddenly taken from this life. • *Gustavian Weekly,* November 15, 1938

THE FIRE Shortly after midnight on the morning of January 8, 1970, fire broke out in the Auditorium, built in 1905. The "Aud" was one of the oldest and busiest buildings on campus, and its destruction disrupted college activities for months to come.

The outside of the building was brick veneer but almost everything inside was made of wood—the floors, the supporting beams, the ceilings (except for some embossed tin), walls of varnished paneling, the desks, the chairs. Much of the contents, furnishings, and furniture was combustible. About 2:15 a.m., we heard a tinkle from the third floor. The window glass was breaking. • **President Frank Barth**[5]

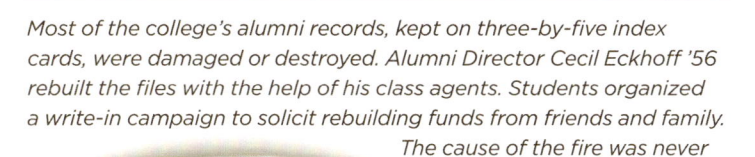

Most of the college's alumni records, kept on three-by-five index cards, were damaged or destroyed. Alumni Director Cecil Eckhoff '56 rebuilt the files with the help of his class agents. Students organized a write-in campaign to solicit rebuilding funds from friends and family. The cause of the fire was never determined.[6]

When I reached campus [a few weeks after the fire] ... I wondered how the gutted building would look. Just four walls rose out of the icy landscape. Cleansed by fire, open to wind and sky, free of their burden of hardwood and plaster, the walls possessed a gaunt beauty that led some to talk of preserving the ruins. But one wall fell that Sunday, so the rest were razed. • **Frank Gamelin '38**[7]

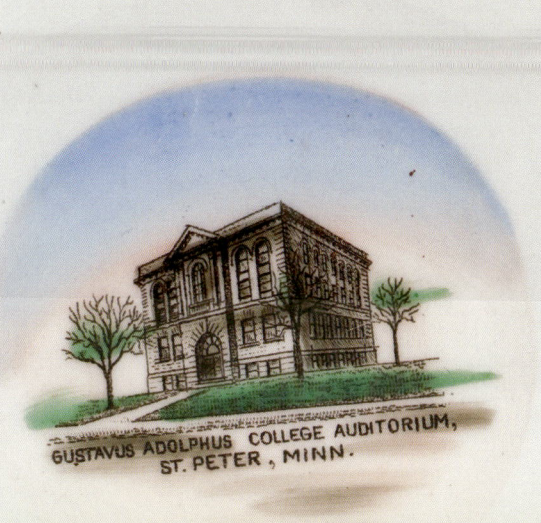

GUSTAVUS ADOLPHUS COLLEGE AUDITORIUM, ST. PETER, MINN.

S STUDY

A saxophone solo cuts through an uncommonly loud late-night commotion in the Market Place.

Faculty, administrators—even President Jack Ohle—don aprons and equip themselves with serving utensils.

A phalanx of streakers wearing only Santa hats races through the library and the Campus Center.

It must be finals week.

Since at least the early 1990s, Gustavus has encouraged its students to take a break on the night before final exams begin—to abandon their books for a couple hours and forget about John Stuart Mill's theories on liberty and Max Planck's quantum hypothesis. Midnight Express, a two-hour carnival of food, music, dance, and campus camaraderie, is designed to serve as a release valve on the end-of-the-semester academic pressure cooker.

The usual lines of authority blur a bit during Midnight Express, as faculty and administrators serve up free helpings of ice cream, soft pretzels, and chicken wings to hundreds of hungry students. But the temporary servers seem to enjoy the experience. "[The students] have all worked hard all semester, and this is our chance to give back to them," says Terena Wilkins, adjunct instructor of theatre and dance. "It's fun to see students outside of class, taking a break from their studies."[1]

It's a break that most students are happy to take. "It just distracts us," says Kari Mlynar '12, whose first final, in Parties and Elections, looms just twelve hours away. "But that's what you need—a distraction. It's awesome. Other schools don't do stuff like this."

For the first hour after the doors open at 10 p.m., the Market Place hums with the energy emitted by hundreds of highly caffeinated Gusties. But as the clock ticks toward midnight, the crowd thins. The break was nice, but now it's time to **study**. The library will remain open for a couple more hours. After that, there's always the study lounge in the dorm. Kari Mlynar, for one, is ready to get it over with. "Oh yeah, I'm fine," she says. "Happens every year. You can't avoid it."[2]

BELOW: *President Jack Ohle and his wife, Kris, serve up chicken wings at the December 2010 Midnight Express.*

It seems that what is supposed to be the seat of learning on our campus has degenerated to another social stamping ground. Not only do students spend hours making dates, breaking dates, discussing profs and other students—all under the guise of "study"—but the main reading room has become an extension of the canteen. Bulging brief cases have been known to house numerous apples, candy bars, cheese sandwiches and maybe even full-course turkey dinners, all of which when chomped upon in a greater or lesser degree of unison add nothing to the academic atmosphere. • *Gustavian Weekly,* **November 14, 1958**

ABOVE, TOP TO BOTTOM: *At the turn of the 19th century, students who did not live on campus—and they constituted the majority—often did their studying in the college's small library, which was located on the second floor of Old Main.*

The first Folke Bernadotte Memorial Library (now the Anderson Social Science Center) was named in honor of Swedish diplomat Count Folke Bernadotte, who was assassinated while serving as the United Nations mediator in Palestine. The library opened in 1948 and immediately became a favorite place to study—and socialize.

The focal point of study shifted yet again when the second Folke Bernadotte Library opened in 1972.

---S---

We all need some kind of study break and some take it by simply closing their eyes for a few minutes. Unfortunately, for some those few minutes can stretch into an hour or longer. But maybe that's okay too—we need that time every now and then to relax and for some the library is more conducive to relaxation than others.

• • •

1984 *Gustavian*

The casual observer may call the college library ugly for it has stark, mean and powerful lines, but such lines are common to fortresses. The library is like an armory where we "repair" to secure the proper weaponry for the battles of life.

• Karl Ozolins, chief librarian, 1974[4]

81

STUDY

When ice cream grows on macaroni trees,
When Sahara's sands are muddy,
When cats and dogs wear BVDs
That's the time I like to study.

• 1927 *Gustavian*

Campus cartoonist Eben Lawson immortalized the study habits of Amy Johnson '25.

In the dormitories, desks have been cleared of the usual debris of letters, cards, coke bottles, newspapers, bobby pins, cuff links, and the general array of miscellaneous articles present the rest of year, and in their place you see strange objects like books, a cup of coffee and "No-doze" pills, and the most surprising of all you find a student there.

***Gustavian Weekly*, May 29, 1959**

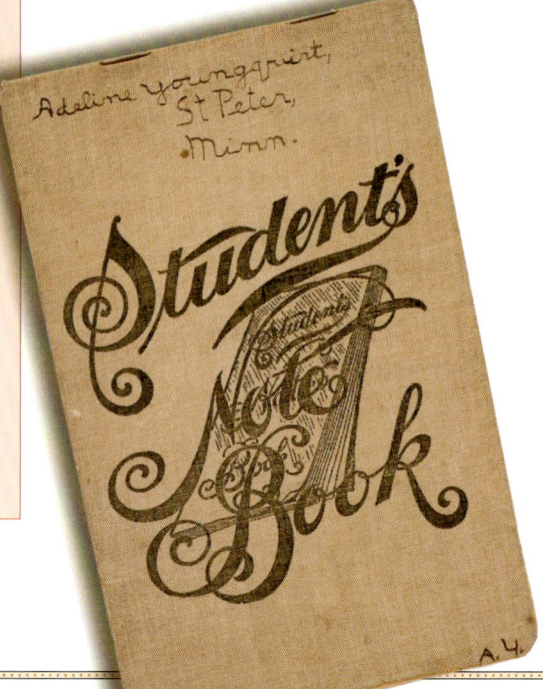

Yes, the advent of semester exams has affected life on the hill. For the unprepared, it is a cause of great fear and trembling; for the diligent, it is a stimulant to increased study and learning; for the campus butterfly, it is a major factor in the decline and fall of the Gustavus social life. For all—it is a necessary and integral part of obtaining a college education. • *Gustavian Weekly,* **February 12, 1960**

Cramming in the Commerce Hall library, probably 1940s.

The fateful first day of finals arrives and miraculously, we somehow survive it in one piece. By the last day of finals, studying is fruitless . . . Finally, the exams are over and Gusties scatter far and wide for vacation and many think to themselves two weeks later, "What was on that exam I worried about so much anyway?" • **1984** *Gustavian*

The caption that ran with this 1962 cartoon read, simply, "Good Luck On Finals!"[3]

Studying in comfort in the Student Union's Linner Lounge, 1957.

S | STUDY

The first Folke Bernadotte Library, opened in 1948.

TOWN

Sophomore John Malmborg '61 and his roommate, Paul Anderson '62, were, like many Gusties during the late 1950s, bored with the meals served at the college's Uhler Hall cafeteria. "Evelyn Young made good food," John recalled years later, "but it was the same thing every day." More and more often, the two roommates were abandoning campus to catch a bite somewhere else. Their favorite restaurant was a place in Mankato that served an exotic dish found nowhere else in the area—pizza. Malmborg and Anderson loved pizza. And then, during the spring semester of 1959, it hit them:

Why not open a pizza joint in St. Peter?

On the evening of September 5, 1959, St. Peter's newest restaurant, the Pizza Villa, opened for business on Minnesota Avenue. Malmborg and Anderson had built the place on the cheap. The décor included black walls, fishnets from Lake Superior, and repainted road construction lanterns procured by a kleptomaniacal friend. The menu featured several pizzas aimed directly at Gustavus stomachs. The Gustaviano Special was topped with "a little bit of everything." The Extra Special—otherwise known as the Sunken Gondola—came with a glass of Alka Selzer on the side. ("It was *really* hot," John laughed.)

The Pizza Villa did "gangbusters" business with Gustavus students, but the people who lived in **town** initially shied away. Many of them had never eaten pizza before and were reluctant to try. It wasn't until a couple years later, when Malmborg (who had, by then, bought out Anderson) introduced broasted chicken, that the restaurant caught on with the locals.

Even with the addition of chicken, the Pizza Villa remained one of the rare businesses in St. Peter that depended primarily on the patronage of Gustavus students. Malmborg claimed that on some nights, his drivers—most of whom were Gusties—made hundreds of deliveries to campus. Malmborg left the pizza business in 1972, but the Pizza Villa continued to operate under different owners into the 1990s.[1]

LEFT: *The Pizza Villa, at its second location on Minnesota Avenue, 1970s.*

In the early decades of the 20th century, Gustavus students called Swanbeck's Restaurant "the place we all go in St. Peter."

"Welcome Gusties!" is a sign which greeted all Gustavians on their first visit to downtown St. Peter last fall. For many this symbolized the store owner's appreciation for the business he would get from the returning college students. Tyron Steen, pharmacist at Swedberg's Drug Store, said that it is his belief, as well as an impression he's gotten from the other businessmen in town, that students are a "definite asset" to their businesses. • *Gustavian Weekly,* April 28, 1972

The B&M Grill was a popular student hangout during the 1950s.

SIGH… THE FLAME MAKES ME HAPPY!!!

Several generations of Gusties have made the Flame Bar a perennial student favorite. The Flame first opened its doors in 1953 and has stayed in business—under a succession of owners—ever since. In recent years, other popular hangouts including Patrick's and Whiskey River have competed for students' affections.[2]

The dining room of St. Peter's Nicollet Hotel. "The Nic's" adjacent bar was known as "Gusties' home away from home" during the 1970s and 1980s.[3]

Slip into a **Bradley** and out-of-doors
$5 $7.50 $10
Sold Exclusively in St. Peter at the
Nutter Clothing Co.

TOWN

Gustavus's ancestral homes: Swedish Lutheran Church in Red Wing, where Eric Norelius opened his school for Swedish immigrants in 1862 (above); and St. Ansgar's Academy in East Union, which operated from 1863 to 1876 (right).

This cartoon, which appeared in the 1904 yearbook, Manhem, depicted the struggle to determine whether Gustavus would stay in St. Peter or move to Minneapolis. St. Peter eventually won, and once again, the financial support of the local community was a crucial factor.

St. Peter with the Gustavus campus in the background, about 1905.

St. Peter is in many ways preferable to the larger cities as a college location. The city, not being very large, naturally does not present the innumerable temptations of a larger place. The students are not subjected to poor air and unhealthy odors, which are so prevalent in larger cities. • *Annual Messenger* (literary circle publication), 1891

> With the return of the students of Gustavus Adolphus College, the citizens of St. Peter feel an interest and enthusiasm which is not dominated by selfish motives. We welcome the students because we not only regard them as members of St. Peter's family, but in reality an integral part of our community life.
> - *Gustavian Weekly,* September 16, 1934

> Gustavus and St. Peter get things solved. They might disagree but they get together. They're like brothers who might differ among themselves, but they stand up for each other. • Bob Wettergren '43, St. Peter businessman[4]

In a display of town-gown unity, contingents of Gustavus students and faculty members left campus to help their St. Peter neighbors rebuild in the aftermath of the 1998 tornado.

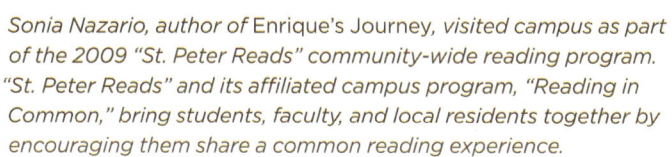

> This is where we live, this is our town, even if it is for just four years. I'm just happy to be able to do something for the town [after the 1998 tornado].
> • Gus Lindquist '98, student volunteer[5]

Sonia Nazario, author of Enrique's Journey, visited campus as part of the 2009 "St. Peter Reads" community-wide reading program. "St. Peter Reads" and its affiliated campus program, "Reading in Common," bring students, faculty, and local residents together by encouraging them share a common reading experience.

U US

Nadvia Davis '11 remembers quite clearly the day she was pulled out of class during her senior year at Minneapolis North High School. She found herself sitting in the guidance office with two men she had never met before. They introduced themselves as Virgil Jones and Eric Coleman from Gustavus Adolphus College.

"And I said, 'Where is that?'" she laughs.

Jones and Coleman had come to North High to recruit Nadvia and one of her classmates. Nadvia had never seriously considered Gustavus. She had her eye on several other schools including one historically black university, Howard, in Washington, DC. But she was willing to listen to what Jones and Coleman had to say. And the more she listened, the more she warmed to the idea of attending school in St. Peter. She enrolled as first-year student at Gustavus in the fall of 2007.

Gustavus has never attracted large numbers of racially underrepresented students, but it has actively recruited them for more than half a century. The effort began slowly in the 1950s and then picked up momentum during the early 1960s when the college started recruiting black students from southern high schools. Black enrollment peaked during the 1970–71 school year and then tailed off as funding for recruitment dried up. But the hard work of diversifying the "**us**" that is Gustavus has continued ever since.

During the winter of her senior year at Gustavus, Nadvia attended a Martin Luther King Jr. Day luncheon with two alumni—Otis Zanders '77 and Lucy (Nelson) Zanders '77—who came to Gustavus from Mississippi and Tennessee in 1973. She listened to their stories of what the college was like back then—how they and their friends in the Black Student Organization helped each other thrive on a campus where they constituted a tiny minority. Nadvia's encounter with the Zanders convinced her that Gustavus is making progress. "They made me realize that this place is changing by the day when it comes to recruiting minority students," she says. "As long as the college puts forth a conscious effort, it'll grow. It's just a matter of time."[1]

Nadvia Davis at Commencement 2011

A sampling of Andersons (Esther, Raymond, and Roger) and Johnsons (Pearl, Raymond, and Victoria) from the Gustavus Class of 1927.

Never before in the history of the school have the blondes and the blue eyes joined to defend the prestige of the land of the midnight sun as [they do today].... Standing foremost in the army of Gustavus Adolphus is the flower of the school, forty and four answering to the call of Anderson. But their brightness is closely rivaled by the unheralded arrival of fifteen tall and short, scrawny and bow-legged, but all straw thatched Johnsons. Altogether there are forty-three sons of John [at Gustavus]. • **Gustavian Weekly, October 11, 1927**

Let men measure their mental abilities with the fair sex, [and] there will be less match-making, less of lovemaking, a better moral atmosphere, better manners, better work.
• Matthias Wahlstrom, president, 1881–1904[3]

For many years, Gustavus's chief claim to diversity was rooted in its firmly established commitment to "co-education."

U US

Gustavus began the slow process of diversifying its student body in the 1920s and 1930s with the admission of at least two students with physical disabilities. Louis Towley '25 (left) had contracted polio as a child and attended Gustavus in a wheelchair. Claire Hobart '35 (right) was a talented pianist who lost his eyesight during childhood.

"Gustavus is really swell. The students are wonderful and the friendliest I've ever encountered." Those are the comments of Chuck Easter, freshman from Albert Lea. Chuck is attending Gustavus on a negro scholarship that has been set up by the Student Senate.

- *Gustavian Weekly,* September 29, 1950

Chuck Easter '54 was the first in a succession of students from minority groups who helped diversify Gustavus's student body during the 1950s.

THEN In the early 1960s, President Edgar Carlson '30 launched an initiative to bring more African American students to Gustavus. Admissions counselor Bruce Gray '61 headed up the effort, making numerous recruiting trips to Chicago and southern states.

Bill "Shorty" Patterson '58, a standout basketball recruit from Minneapolis, was one of the top Gustavus athletes of the 1950s.

Bruce Gray '61 and some of his African American recruits at a 1988 reunion of Gustavus's Black Student Organization (BSO).

Spurred by a steady increase in black enrollment during the 1960s, African American students at Gustavus formed the Black Student Organization, a group dedicated to "preserving the god-given strength for unity in the Black family." [2]

> *Our being here has done a lot for black people. We've proven what really didn't have to be proved—that we can do just as well as white students.*
> • Talmadge King '70[4]

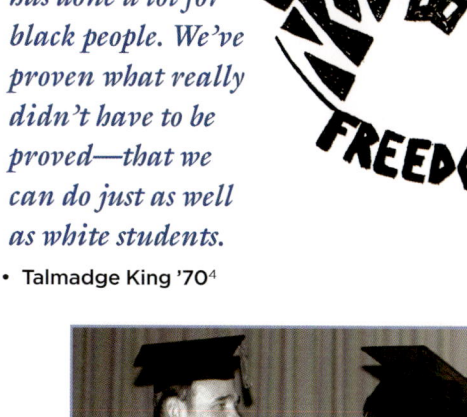

After graduating from Gustavus in 1973, Phil Bryant returned to campus 16 years later to teach in the Department of English.

NOW Through a variety of organizations and initiatives, Gustavus continues to build on the multicultural momentum that began gathering on campus a half century ago.

> *We need not fear that diversity will somehow dilute our sense of community. . . . While similarity of purpose, mission, and of vision, as well as of basic values, are integral to community rightly so called, diversity in all forms of nature and artifice is something to be desired, something to be sought, something to be celebrated.* • Axel Steuer, Gustavus president, 1991–2002[6]

ABOVE, CLOCKWISE FROM UPPER LEFT: *Building Bridges, Asian Cultures Club, Queers & Allies, Diversity Center*

VARSITY

For the first time in its 92-year history, the Gustavus Adolphus men's **varsity** basketball team was playing for a national championship. The 2003 Gusties had clawed their way through the post season, surprising a string of heavily favored opponents including Whitworth, Wisconsin–Stevens Point, Hanover, and Hampden-Sydney in the NCAA Division III Tournament. Now just one team stood in their way: the Ephs of Williams College. Nearly 300 Gustavus faithful had endured a 20-hour bus ride to be on hand for the championship game at the Civic Center in Salem, Virginia. They had come to witness history. Some were even throwing around the word "destiny."

The Gusties held the lead for more than 39 minutes after the opening tip-off. But with less than a minute left, the game turned into a back-and-forth nail-biter. The Ephs took their first lead, 64–63, with just 47 seconds left on the clock. Then Gustavus went back ahead 65–64 with a clutch basket. As the seconds ticked away, the game came down to free throws. The Ephs made one. Then two more. Final score: 67–64.[1]

During the ceremony that followed, every member of the Gustavus team made a point of shaking the hand of each Williams player who won an individual award. That display of sportsmanship left a lasting impression. "[It] was the most noticed and commented-on act of the entire tournament," a Williams parent wrote in letter to Gustavus Coach Mark Hanson. "[Your players] are wonderful representatives of your college and a lot of people . . . will remember the qualities your team showed us all this past weekend."[2]

Hanson and his players were devastated by the loss, but they demonstrated uncommon class in defeat. "What our guys did was not routine," Hanson said. "It wasn't required. It wasn't expected. It wasn't the protocol. That it came after a disappointing loss, showed a level of character that may not have been unique, but it was special. It showed great respect for the event they were in to say, 'We hate to have lost this, but congratulations.'"[3]

BELOW: *Members of the 2003 Gustavus men's basketball team gather with their supporters after the championship game trophy presentation in Salem, Virginia.*

FIRSTS Gustavus's tradition of intercollegiate athletics began during the 1902–3 school year, with men's football, women's basketball, and men's baseball leading the way. But the sudden burst of athletic competition was short lived. In 1905, the College—acting under a directive from the Lutheran Augustana Synod—banned all intercollegiate sports competition. Five years later, the ban was lifted on all sports except football. In 1917, the football ban was lifted, too. The stage was set for a new era of athletic accomplishments at Gustavus.

November 6, 1902
First intercollegiate football game
Gustavus 11, Mankato Normal 6

February 14, 1903
First intercollegiate basketball game
Mankato Normal 16, Gustavus 2

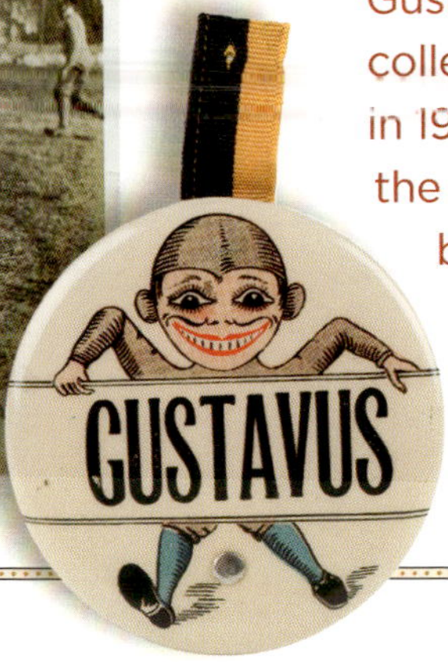

April 20, 1903
First intercollegiate baseball game
St. Olaf 17, Gustavus 1

After many attempts and appeals by the students, faculty and friends of Gustavus, the ruling [prohibiting intercollegiate football] was abolished . . . in 1917. . . . All true Gustavians received the news of this action with great joy because that would make it possible for the grand old school to send her pigskin warriors on the gridiron again. • **1920** *Gustavian*

VARSITY

CONFERENCE PLAY In the first 20 years after the founding of the Minnesota Intercollegiate Athletic Conference (MIAC) in 1920, Gustavus won 32 championships. Its titles were spread among nine sports: football, basketball, baseball, track, golf, tennis, gymnastics, hockey, and swimming.

1938 Hockey

1932 Gymnastics

1927 Swimming

1920s Track and Field

THE "GOLDEN FIFTIES" The "Golden Fifties" were a decade of triumph for Gustavus. The football team won eight conference championships; the basketball team won three; and the swimming team six.

1955 Gustavus backfield (L-R): Don Roberts '56, Jim Knight '55, Mike McInerny '55, and Don Hauskens '56

1954 Basketball

WOMEN'S VARSITY Gustavus's women athletes had stopped competing on the intercollegiate level in 1920. But women's sports rebounded in the early 1960s when Gustavus began developing a women's gymnastics program—one of the first in the Upper Midwest. Other women's programs, including basketball and volleyball, soon followed.

Coach Steve Wilkinson (far right) with his 1980 national championship team.

Gymnast Sally Grubb, 1967

1975 Hockey

1972 Basketball ("the Bees")

WIDESPREAD SUCCESS In the 1960s and 1970s, Gustavus began establishing itself as a powerhouse in a wide range of sports including hockey (12 MIAC championships between 1966 and 1978) and tennis (two NCAA Division III titles in 1980 and 1982).

HIGH RANKINGS In recent years, Gustavus's athletics program has amassed one of the most impressive overall records of accomplishment in Division III. In 2011 it ranked third among all NCAA schools in the number of student athletes earning NCAA Postgraduate Scholarships; seventh all-time among Division III schools in the number of Academic All-Americans; and tenth in Division III in the number of NCAA championship appearances over the previous ten years.

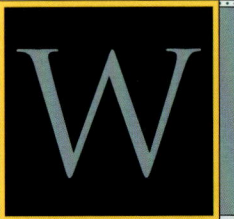

WELCOME

Matthew "Chooey" Wasson '12 and his fellow "Gustie Greeters" have staked out a spot on Ring Road, just south of the heating plant. It is now impossible for any vehicle attempting to deliver an incoming first-year to the Sohre or Pittman residence halls to make the journey without first running a gauntlet of incredibly enthusiastic type-A personalities. It is first-year student move-in day, 2010—otherwise known as "Greeter Christmas."

A grey sedan turns onto the road and heads the greeters' way.

"Here we go!"

Chooey and the other greeters crank up a choreographed cheer. The sedan slows to a crawl. Hoots. Hollers. Clapping. Whistles. The wide-eyed first-year in the passenger seat is laughing. The driver—dad, apparently—gives a wave and proceeds on toward Sohre.

Not just anyone can be a Gustie Greeter. This year, about 90 students applied to join the greeter corps. Only 25 were chosen. Selection is a three-stage weeding out process during which candidates are judged not only on their enthusiasm, but also on their ability to handle just about any issue that might confront a first-year student—from caf account snafus, to roommate problems, to dropping a class. Those who make the cut go through a weeklong training session before the first-years arrive. Greeters have to be ready to do much more than greet.

This is Chooey's second move-in day as a Gustie Greeter. The role seems to fit him well. Like most greeters, he decided his first day on campus that this might be his Gustavus calling. "When I got on the hill and I was coming up College Avenue and I saw these people jumping around in lion costumes, just to make me feel **welcome**, it was a great feeling," he says. "It was a lot of fun and I knew I wanted to do that. I just hoped at the time that I had the personality to do it."[1]

BELOW: *Matthew "Chooey" Wasson '12 and his Gustie Greeter compatriots welcome another first-year to campus.*

Freshman-Senior picnic, 1958

ORIENTATION The late 1950s ushered in the end of what the *Gustavian Weekly* called "the paddle-smacking, egg-smearing era" of first-year orientation.[2] Hazing was out. Mentoring was in. Upper-class volunteers known as "Big Wheels," "Good Guys," and, later, "Gustie Greeters" helped their first-year counterparts survive and enjoy their first weeks on campus.

Dear Mom,

After you and Dad left me and my baggage here on the Hill in St. Peter last Thursday, strange things have been happening. For instance Thursday night we had a watermelon bust. I didn't eat much watermelon but I had a lot of fun holding hands with the girls.

- Dick Knutson '62[3]

President Jack Ohle and a contingent of Gustie Greeters teach first-year students the "Gustie Rouser" at the President's Banquet during new student orientation, 2009.

* GUSTIE ROUSER *

Come on you Gusties, Fight on, Fight on
Shout out the battle cry of victory
Come on you Gusties, Fight to the end
Fight on for dear ol' G.A.C.

Gusties will shine tonight, Gusties will shine!
Gusties will shine tonight, Gusties will shine!
Gusties will shine tonight, Gusties will shine!

Beat 'em, Bust 'em, That's our custom
Gusties will shine!

Gustie Greeters line up for one of the highlights of new student orientation—the candlelight service in Christ Chapel.

Author Jamie Ford signs copies of his book, Hotel on the Corner of Bitter and Sweet, *the 2010 "Reading in Common" selection for first-year students.*

W | WELCOME

MOVE-IN DAY Nearly every student who has ever attended Gustavus has begun his or her college career in the same way—by moving into a dorm. The process usually follows a predictable pattern: carry in all your stuff; meet your new roommate; and, finally, say goodbye to the people who brought you.

—W—

Equipped with everything from electric sun lamps to massive stuffed animals, we marched bravely up the steps of our new homes and tried not to flinch when confronted with the realization that the cute closets in Wahlstrom were to be our rooms for the next nine months.

•••

Judy Langkos '63[4]

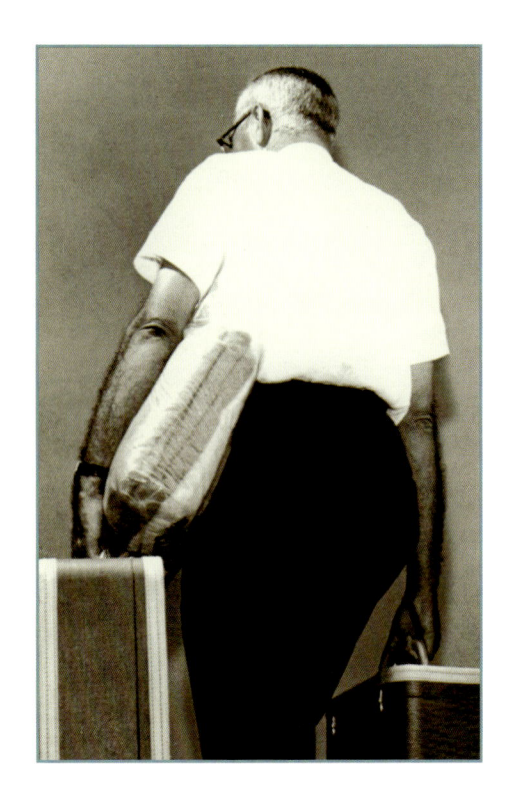

INITIATION In the days before "Big Wheels," "Good Guys," and "Gustie Greeters," first-year students at Gustavus often thought of upperclassmen as tormentors, not mentors. Being a freshman meant wearing a green beanie, performing humiliating tasks, and facing the prospect of painful punishment should you fail to obey your "betters."

> All freshmen will be privileged to wear their freshman green beanies at all times and at all places. This includes the active hours spent in class, the shower, and off campus, etc., and the immobile hours spent in the sack. The only exception is that freshman boys shall not wear beanies entering, during, or leaving chapel.
>
> "Honors and Privileges Bestowed Upon the Lowly Freshman Class by the Great and Noble Senior Class of 1955"[5]

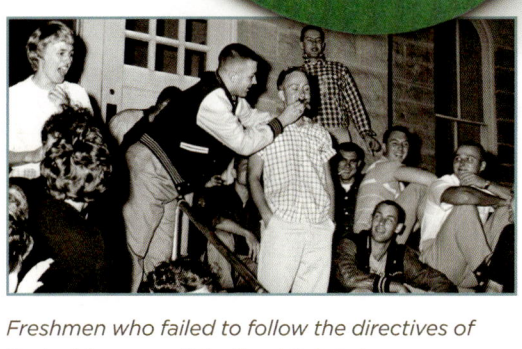

Freshmen who failed to follow the directives of their elders were "tried" publicly in kangaroo courts, where punishment was meted out on the spot.

WELCOME BACK Arriving first-year students are not the only beneficiaries of Gustavus hospitality. Over the decades, the Gustavus community has gone out of its way to welcome back alumni and their families during Homecoming and other campus-wide events.

LEFT: *The Class of 1920 returns to campus for its silver anniversary in the spring of 1945.*
RIGHT: *20-year homecoming reunion photo of the Class of 1988.*

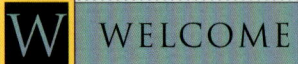

WELCOME

102

The freshman-sophomore tug-o-war—complete with water cannons—was a regular feature of faculty-supervised field days during the 1920s.

X CHROMOSOMES

There has always been a certain segment of the Gustavus student body that enjoys monitoring fashion trends on campus. While many Gusties are disinclined—whether through lack of interest or lack of funds—to spend much time thinking about wardrobes and grooming, others take fashion seriously. And serious or not, the choices they make often reflect the times in which they live.

Over the years, Gusties with two **X chromosomes** have frequently been judged—by men and by other women—on the basis of their looks. In an early example of this phenomenon, an alumnus from the Class of 1901 described his female classmates as unnatural beauties with "wasp waists" who hid themselves behind "hideous . . . street-sweeping skirts and reinforced high collars."[1]

The daring flapper styles of the 1920s bypassed campus, but by the late 1930s, many Gustavus women were adopting a more casual look. "Co-eds" were showing up in class—and even chapel—wearing "slacks" instead of skirts, and some Gusties were appalled. "We're not saying that it isn't fine to be unconventional occasionally," Marjorie Knudson '42 tut-tutted, "but isn't it just a bit sloppy . . . careless, and even rude to the profs and classmates?"[2] By the early 1950s jeans were becoming more common. A few years later, a pair of self-appointed campus style watchers raised alarms about another trend: Bermuda shorts:

There was a co-ed called Gertruda
She got some shorts from Bermuda
They caused a sensation
All over the nation
Perhaps you can wear them—She shouldn'ta.[3]

The 1960s and 1970s introduced new apparel trends (think mini-skirts and cut-offs) that would have scandalized earlier generations of fashion police. By the 1980s, many Gustie women were mimicking the styles seen at East Coast prep schools—especially Izod polo shirts with their trademark crocodile logo. (Standard campus joke: "Kill a preppy, save an alligator.")[4] Over the last two decades, casual dress—including college-licensed "Gustie Gear"—has prevailed. Among the most recent, and sometimes controversial trends: leggings. (In the words of *Weekly* columnist Susan Kranz '11, "Leggings equate pants? No!")[5] Styles may change, but the urge to pass judgment on them remains as strong as ever.

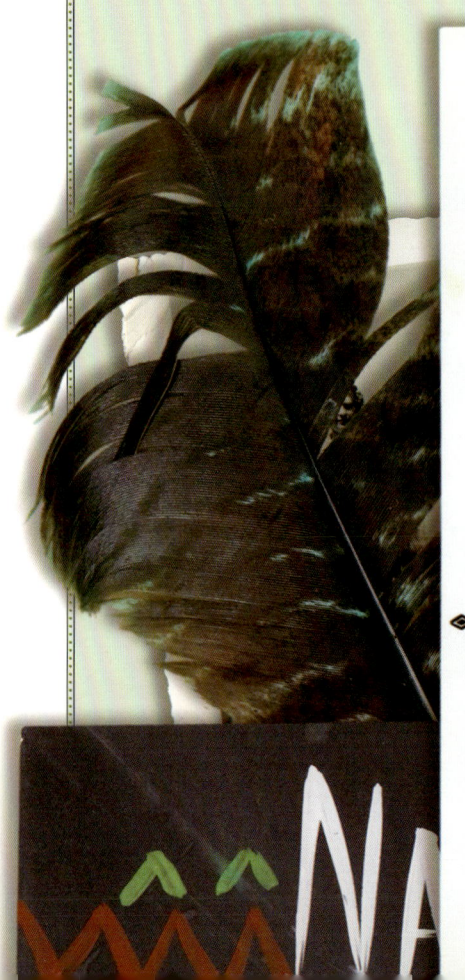

WOMANHOOD For many years, women were in the minority at Gustavus. Now they account for a majority of the student body. As their numbers have grown, so too have their ambitions. At one time, the jokes about female Gusties seeking "MRS" degrees reflected a certain reality. But that reality began to change for good during the 1970s.

Listen loud and clear men: women do not belong to you. Think of us not as a toy that you can play with but more like the weather—uncontrollable, sometimes pleasant, sometimes violent, but in all cases not up to you. • Natasha Hawkins '07, 2005[6]

— X —

During 1975, International Women's Year, females celebrated their liberation from a strictly male world. What did it mean for the Gustavus Frau? . . . The unanswered questions of womanhood will remain unanswered until all women discover a sense of self-worth and begin to recognize themselves as independent beings, and not identified by their relationship with a man.

. . .

1976 *Gustavian*

Here she comes—another co-ed. She has just finished some toast and coffee at Cook's Café and now she is bound, via the laundry, for the city library . . . She never skips gym. She will graduate among the upper third, receive a high recommendation, and will go out to teach biology and physical education in the Powder Prairie High School. She helps to make the world a brighter and happier place to live in. She is the modern girl. The world needs her.

• *Gustavian Weekly,* December 1, 1925

X CHROMOSOMES

SORORITIES The sororities at Gustavus date back to 1904, when two "literary societies—or "ladies' societies"—were formed. The first one was called "Independent Blessings," or, more commonly, the "IBs." The IBs officially changed their name to Iota Beta in 1922. The second was TMT, ostensibly named after the initials found on the group's skeleton mascot. TMT was also known by various nicknames such as "The Modest Ten" and "The Modest Tribe." It adopted the Greek letters Tau Mu Tau around 1930 and today ranks as the oldest active sorority on campus.

An early portrait of Gustavus's first sorority, the IBs. The scrapbook in which this photo appears includes the notation, "Independent Blessings in name, Nuisances in fact."

Like many sororities at Gustavus, the TMTs adopted an identifying group persona—in their case, "Indians."

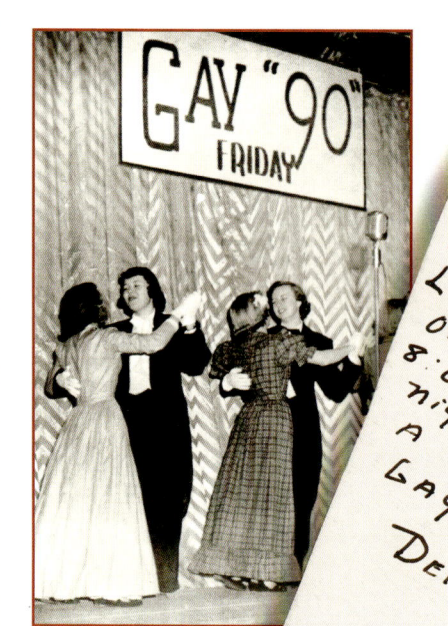

Delta Phi Omega rush party, 1951

Sigma Sigma Sigma, Gustavus's first nationally affiliated sorority, 2009

[The stock phrase] "Thank you ma'am, please may I have another?" pleaded seventy-two pledges to their pledgemasters at their nightly "board meetings" during sorority initiation activities this past week. Shrill screams, sorority songs sung backwards and forwards, and the sharp cracking sound of busy paddles echoed out from the Wahlstrom laundry rooms at these nightly sessions.

• *Gustavian Weekly,* **October 17, 1952**

WOMEN'S ORGANIZATIONS Although sororities have been active at Gustavus for more than a century, other women's groups have contributed to campus life as well. In the years before Title IX, the Women's Athletic Association (later, the Women's Recreation Association) encouraged female students to stay physically active. The Association of Women Students (AWS), which originally devoted itself mostly to social functions, transformed into an issues-based organization in the early 1970s. AWS folded in 1977 and was replaced a new group that has since gone by several names including the Women's Referral Service, the Women's Center, and the Womyn's Awareness Center.

Women's Recreation Association, 1970s

There are women at Gustavus who are interested in areas and issues beyond those with which the sororities and AWS [Association of Women Students] are presently concerned. There are Gustavus women interested in job opportunities, interested in birth control information, interested in a larger world than that of teas and style shows. We question whether these women are being represented by their own women's organizations. • **Gustavian Weekly,** October 16, 1970

Women's athletics, 1940s-style.

Marty Daly of the Association of Women Students uses a rubber duck to make a point about birth control, 1971.

A Wednesday evening gathering at the Womyn's Awareness Center, 2010.

Y CHROMOSOMES

Anyone who believes that Gustavians with **Y chromosomes** have never cared much about their clothes or appearance should consider the following account. In an article that appeared in a 1926 edition of the *Gustavian Weekly*, an unidentified alumnus described the wardrobe he brought to campus as a freshman in 1897. It included:

Two suits: "one best and one not so good."

Two pairs of shoes: "a pair of patent leathers . . . and a pair of yellow oxfords."

"A brown, high-crowned, narrow-brimmed derby hat with two brass-lined holes on each side for ventilation."

"A white shirt with a stiffly-starched shield-shaped bosom."

And finally, "a collar of the choker variety . . . set off with a ready-tied four-in-hand cravat."[1]

During the first 75 years or so of Gustavus's history, men on campus were expected to dress well. Men's clothing stores in St. Peter such as Haesecke's and Nutter's enticed college customers with ads for everything from suits and ties to "Playboy" handkerchiefs to "Everwear" stockings ("the choice of men who dress with distinction.")[2]

Expectations that men would wear "proper attire" began fading in the 1930s with the onset of the Great Depression. T-shirts (including the first ones sporting Gustavus logos) and denim jeans soon became wardrobe essentials. By the early 1940s, the typical Gustavus male had abandoned most sartorial pretenses. "Shirttails are set like sails to aid locomotion," one campus fashion critic observed. "On the other hand, one may be greeted with an array of grey sweatshirts of indistinguishable age, obviously one-time possessions of the athletic department."[3]

In the years since World War II, casual attire has become the norm among men on campus. Although many male Gusties have been known to keep suits or sport coats in their closets, they usually "dress up" only in emergencies—such as the President's Ball. From the cut-off jeans of the 1970s to the trucker hats of the 2000s, male fashion trends at Gustavus are almost always of the "dressed down" variety. The days when a typical freshman's wardrobe included two suits and a "four-in-hand cravat" are long gone.

MANHOOD Browse through back issues of the *Gustavian Weekly* and you will find descriptions of nearly every male type imaginable: the bookworm; the slob; the preacher's kid; the lady's man; the frat boy; the jock. These and other "typical" males have always been present at Gustavus in one form or another, but every young man who comes to the campus in St. Peter has to decide for himself whether "typical" is enough.

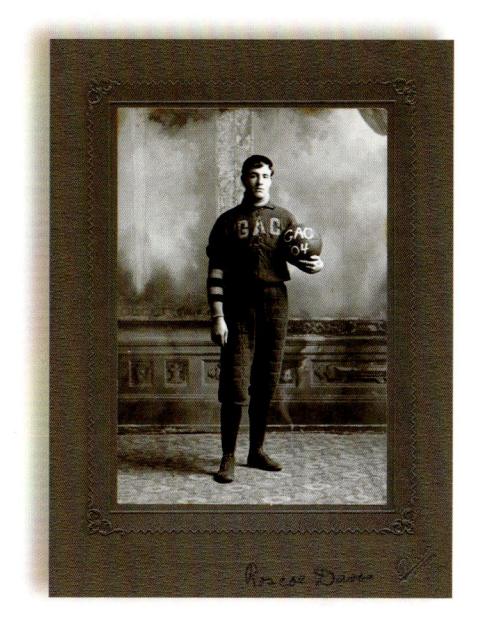

What do I think of Gustavus men? I like them! . . . Improve some of the table manners exhibited in the caf, teach a handful of them that gentlemen still do give up their seats in crowded buses—and you'll have a hard time beating Gustavus men anywhere! • *Gustavian Weekly,* January 9, 1940

The beard-growing contest was a regular feature of Frost Weekends during the fifties and sixties.

When you're a freshman guy at Gustavus you have it pretty easy. You stumble around campus for the first six or eight weeks and no one really pays attention to you. Judging by the typical behavior exhibited by a freshman male that's probably just as well.

• 1976 *Gustavian*

Y CHROMOSOMES

FRATERNITIES Fraternities got their start at Gustavus in 1906, with the formation of a secret society officially called "Turbescon" and popularly known as "T.C.O.S." or the "Reds." Four years later a rival society called the "Grays" formed to challenge the Reds' social dominance on campus. After several years in administration-imposed exile, both societies reorganized as chartered fraternities. The Reds became Tau Psi Omega and the Greys became Nu Upsilon Gamma. Meanwhile, several other fraternities including the "Alphs" (Phi Alpha), the "Eppies" (Epsilon Pi Alpha), the "Chieftains" (Chi Iota Kappa), "OKs" (Omega Kappa), and "Sigs" (Kappa Sigma Chi) grew out of recognized debating societies. The fraternity culture at Gustavus remained strong until 1988 when the College banned all Greek organizations in the wake of fraternity hazing violations. Fraternities (and sororities) were reinstated in 1993 and have since reestablished their importance to campus life.

Alphs, 1962

The Grays in 1910 (right) and more than a half-century later (below)

> It won't be long now before there will resound from the walls of the campus the steady beat of the paddle accompanied by the groans and wails of some of those pledges who have thus far come in contact with only the more pleasant portions of fraternity life.
> • *Gustavian Weekly,* April 13, 1937

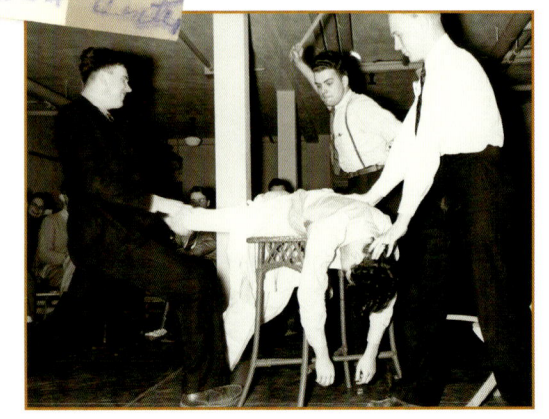

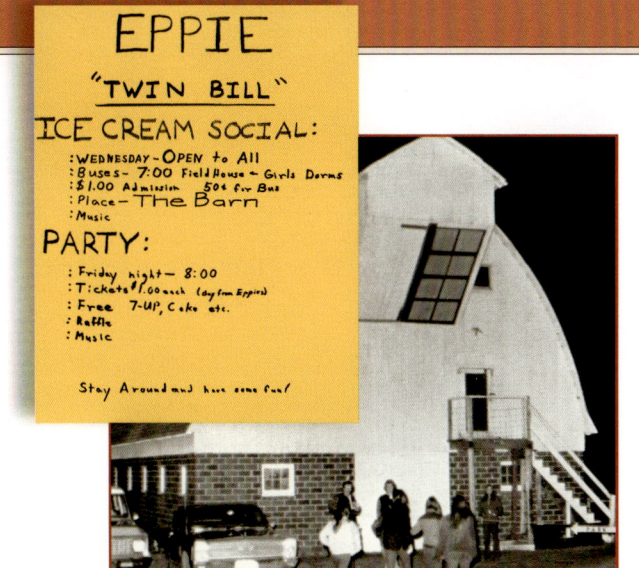

EPPIE

"TWIN BILL"

ICE CREAM SOCIAL:
- WEDNESDAY - OPEN to All
- Buses - 7:00 Field House + Girls Dorms
- $1.00 Admission 50¢ for Bus
- Place - The Barn
- Music

PARTY:
- Friday night - 8:00
- Tickets $1.00 each (buy from Eppie)
- Free 7-UP, Coke etc.
- Raffle
- Music

Stay Around and have some fun!

Beginning in the late 1960s, Gustavus's fraternities began sponsoring off-campus parties known as "beer busts" (or, in deference to college administrators, "ice cream socials"). The most popular location for these busts was "The Barn," a privately owned building outside Le Sueur.

SAE (Sigma Alpha Epsilon) is Gustavus's newest frat and the first to be affiliated with the National Interfraternity Conference.

MEN'S ORGANIZATIONS Over the years, most of the organizations catering exclusively to men on campus have been connected either to Greek life or athletics. There have been a few exceptions, however. During World War II, Gustavus hosted a U.S. Navy V-12 unit, which trained hundreds of men entering military service. More recently, a new organization called M-Pact—affiliated with the Center for Vocational Reflection—has provided opportunities for young men to explore the meanings and implications of masculinity in today's world.

For the benefit of those not acquainted with the ruling in regard to the wearing of foreign letters, the "G" Club desires that the following be known: Any letter or insignia other than the official "G" granted by the Gustavus Athletic Board must NOT be worn by any Gustavus student. We appreciate your cooperation in this respect. •

Gustavian Weekly, September 18, 1928

For many years, athletes who earned letters at Gustavus were automatically enrolled in the exclusive "G Club."

Students with the U.S. Navy V-12 unit, which studied and trained at Gustavus during World War II, from 1943 to 1945.

Gustavus President Jack Ohle meets for lunch with student and faculty members of M-Pact, 2010.

Z ZEITGEIST

Ruth Snyder (Larson) started at Gustavus at a particularly inauspicious time—in the fall of 1929. Less than two months after classes began, the U.S. stock market crashed and the economy soon followed. Ruth's four years at Gustavus coincided with the worst years of the Great Depression. Times were hard, on campus and off.

But there was something intangible about Gustavus that helped students like Ruth keep on with their studies while surrounded by economic devastation. With no money to spare and the college in financial straits, Gustavians leaned on each other for support and created their own diversions.

For Ruth, few activities were more diverting than basketball. She lived off campus, without the camaraderie that came with dorm living, so basketball provided a much-needed social outlet. The games were interclass affairs—freshmen versus sophomores, and so on—and the season always ended with a tournament in the old gymnasium. There wasn't much to do on campus during those lean years, so the championship game always drew a big crowd. "Even the boys came to watch when we had those tournaments," Ruth recalled. "That was exciting."

As the women battled in their ungainly uniforms (blouses, jumpers, and bloomers), the student body, tightly packed into the balcony above the court, joined in raucous renditions of their favorite Gustie cheer:

Rockar, stokar, Tor och hans bockar!
Tjor, igenom! Tjor igenom!

The cheer was infectious and nonsensical. Roughly translated from Swedish, it read, in part:

Thor and his goats!
Drive through! Drive through![1]

Maybe it was the spirit of the age—the **zeitgeist**—that allowed Ruth and her friends to endure hard times. But maybe it was something else—a spirit of the place, of Gustavus—that explained their resilience and optimism. It was a spirit that Gustavians of every era could understand, even if they didn't always egg each other on with cheers about goats.[2]

BELOW, LEFT TO RIGHT: *Ruth Larson '33 at her home in St. Peter, 2010*

Gustavus's 1930 intramural basketball champions, including the future Ruth Larson '33 (back row, left) and the future Evelyn Young '33 (front row, left).

1920S Undergraduate friendships are more ideal than those of the world at large. They are accompanied with feelings and emotions which color all associations in a roseate hue. • *Gustavian Weekly,* May 31, 1927

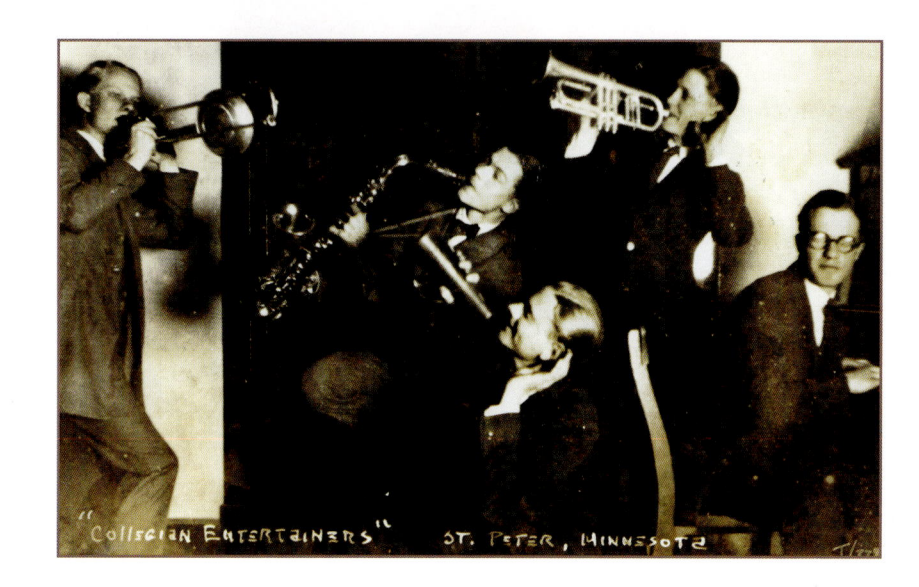

1930S The friendships and associations we have had while in college, even though they may become memories fading into the past as time slips by in its wild rush toward the brink of eternity, will be a source of comfort and inspiration. • *Gustavian Weekly,* June 9, 1931

1940S *To a Navy man, whose home is where he hangs his hat, Gustavus was a real home. The friendliness of the students and the cooperative spirit of the instructors and the administration made that home a happy one.* • Lloyd Reedstrom, V-12 student, 1944[3]

ZEITGEIST

1950S We have here [at Gustavus] an opportunity to meet some of the sincerest and greatest friends we'll ever have.... You might say, we have the prospect of being a member of one of the largest and most productive families in the world! • *Gustavian Weekly,* September 23, 1955

1960S *We are boxed in, lonely, mute, immobilized people . . . but someone down the hall is boxed in, too. Touch him, smell him, hear him, and speak to him, lest your own box becomes narrower and narrower, until it becomes your casket.*
• Robert Esbjornson '41, Department of Religion, 1968[4]

1970S *Aside from books, there are people in college. Understanding them and their ways is as important as being knowledgeable. You can learn from a beer bust like you can learn from a book.* • Brad Hanson '76[5]

1980S *As the years [have flown by], the group of people I call my friends has steadily grown. The excitement of meeting new people doesn't diminish after freshman year. In fact, it may even increase as making friends becomes a special occasion rather than a necessity brought on by not knowing a single person on this campus.* • Tracey Anderson '86[6]

1990S *Never again in our lives will we surround ourselves with the friends that we have made here, nor will the experience ever be quite the same. The friends have been the best, and will be the hardest to leave.* • Steve Lautz '96

2000S *Stop and think about the people who are important in your life at Gustavus, and make time for them. The things we will remember most about college life are not our test scores, class lectures, and library study sessions, but the time we spent with the people who mean the most in our lives.* • Julie Wenaas '06

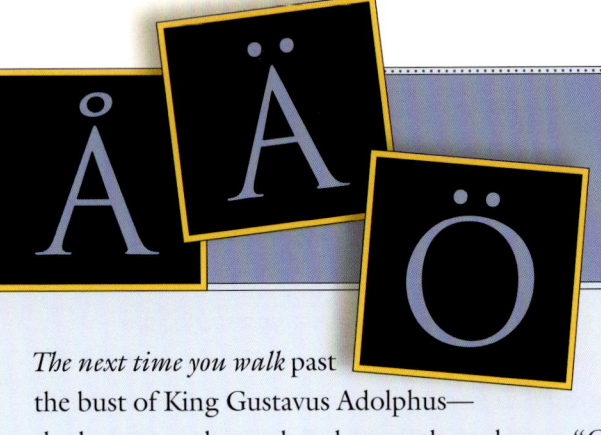

Å Ä Ö

The next time you walk past the bust of King Gustavus Adolphus—the bronze sculpture best known these days as "Gus"—try to imagine what it must have been like to attend its unveiling on November 6, 1932.

It was the 300th anniversary of the Swedish "hero king's" death on the battlefield of Lützen. The sculpture—a replica of a work by a German artist said to be a contemporary of the king—was a gift from Swedish philanthropists who wished to recognize the link between their homeland and the college that Swedish immigrants had founded in Minnesota just 70 years before. Two Gustavus students—Mildred Nelson, representing the United States, and Ruth Knock, representing Sweden—unveiled the statue. The president of the alumni association, W. R. Youngquist, urged the audience to cherish the college's Swedish heritage and honor the man whose name it shared. "We are assembled in the presence of an institution which bears his name and which our fathers have sacrificed to establish and perpetuate," he said. "[We] shall not forget nor fail to appreciate the debt [we] owe this hero."[1]

Fifty-six years earlier, at the dedication of another landmark—Old Main—the college's founder, Eric Norelius, had declared in no uncertain terms that Gustavus's "peculiar claim" was "to reach and educate the Swedish youths of our state."[2] By 1932 the mission had changed. It had been nearly four decades since the majority of a graduating class was Swedish-born.[3] The college had stopped requiring students to take Swedish language classes in 1903. And yet the allure of the "home country" remained strong.

The students, faculty, and alumni who gathered to dedicate the bust of the college's namesake understood the connection between Gustavus and Sweden. Many if not most of them appreciated it. "It's in the bloodstream," an alumnus of the Class of '25 said of his alma mater. "It serves as a unique vitamin, probably vitamin **å**, **ä**, or **ö**, which any fool knows is distilled out of good coffee, *skorpor* [biscuits], *potatis* [potatoes], *korv* [sausage] and *torkad sill* [dried herring].[4]

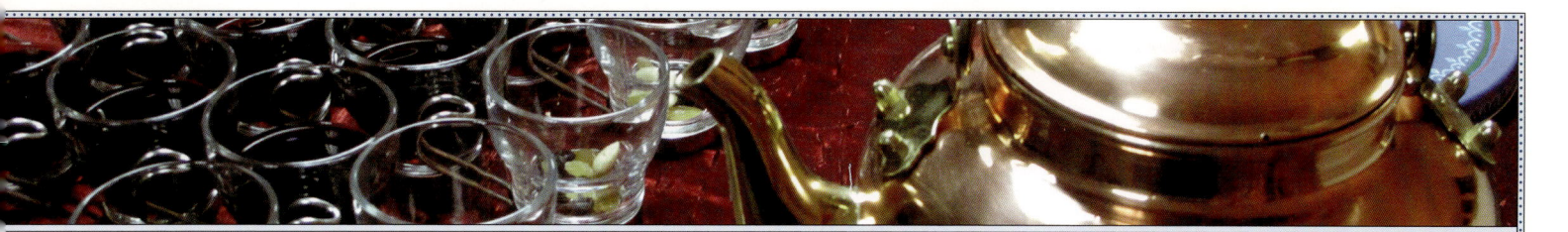

Traditional Swedish glögg at the 2009 President's Christmas Dinner.

HERITAGE From its earliest days, Gustavus has sought to honor its ethnic heritage through symbolic events such as the unveiling of "Gus" and, perhaps most significantly, through its academic program. Swedish language, history, and culture have long been important features of the curriculum. In 1971, they achieved additional prominence with the addition of Scandinavian Area Studies, an interdisciplinary program under the direction of Roland Thorstensson. The program added new faculty including Roger McKnight and Byron Nordstrom, and achieved departmental status in 1982.

Karl Kilander's Swedish class, 1926

Roland Thorstensson, 2010

> [Gustavus] is yet in the mere infancy—it will take time for its growth and development, but I know the spirit of the people that is interested in it, and I cannot doubt that they will stick to it, love and encourage it, and make it a power of good for themselves and indirectly to the whole state.
> - Eric Norelius, Gustavus founder, 1876[5]

Serving line at a midcentury Homecoming smörgåsbord.

The College's Swedish heritage was prominently on display at this gathering in the Auditorium chapel.

Å Ä Ö

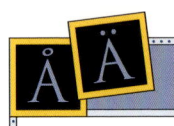

COMING Swedish dignitaries have made a habit of visiting Gustavus over the years.

Archbishop Nathan Söderblom of Sweden came to Gustavus in 1923, seven years before he was awarded the Nobel Peace Prize.

Sweden's Count Folke and Countess Estelle Bernadotte visited Gustavus during the summer of 1933. The college's library would later be named in the count's honor.

[Gustavus] has from the very beginning acted as a bridge between the old country and the new life that the Swedish immigrants and their descendants have formed in America. • **King Carl XVI Gustaf, 1976**[6]

In 1976, Sweden's King Carl XVI Gustaf made his first visit to the Gustavus campus. He returned for two more visits—with Queen Sylvia—in 1982 and 1996.

During a visit to campus in 1979, Sweden's Prince Bertil donned a Gustavus letter sweater that he received as a gift two decades earlier.

Swedish actor Max Von Sydow spent a week on campus as the college's Out of Scandinavia artist-in-residence in 1995.

GOING Sweden has long been one of the most popular study-abroad destinations for Gustavus students.

Linda Wallenberg '75 spent her junior year at Uppsala University in Sweden.

Stockholm City Hall was just one of the stops on the Gustavus Band's 1990 Scandinavian tour.

Alex Legeros '11 in Sweden, 2009

Being of Swedish descent, I have always been interested in Swedish culture and ever since I was young I hoped to study in Sweden one day.... With the help of Gustavus, I have been able to realize that goal. • Linda Wallenberg '75[7]

STAYING Since 1974 students interested in Scandinavian Studies have had the option of living in Swedish House. The old Swedish House, with its distinctive blue and yellow exterior, was damaged beyond repair by the 1998 tornado. Its replacement, part of the International Center, opened in 2000.

Swedish House residents with door salvaged from their former home.

Swedish House, pre-tornado.

Barbro Osher Svenska Huset, the Swedish House in its post-tornado incarnation.

NOTES

GUSTAVUS PERIODICALS
FN .... *Faculty Notes*
GQ .... *Gustavus Quarterly*
Junction .... *Junction* (1971–72)
NOTA .... *None of the Above* (1972–73)
Weekly .... *Gustavian Weekly*

GUSTAVUS YEARBOOKS
Manhem 1904
Runes 1906
Valkyria 1909
Breidablick 1912
Gustavian .... 1917–present (irregular)

NEWSPAPERS
MFP .... *Mankato Free Press*
MST .... *Minneapolis Star Tribune*
MT .... *Minneapolis Tribune*
SPP .... *St. Paul Pioneer Press*

BOOKS
Barth .... Barth, Frank. *A Place Called Gustavus: The Protest Years*. Minneapolis: Primarius Promotion, 2006.

Elvee .... Elvee, Richard. *Gustavus Adolphus College: Kingdom of Identity*. St. Peter: Gustavus Adolphus College, 1987.

Haeuser .... Haeuser, Michael J. *With Grace, Elegance, and Flair: The First 25 Years of Gustavus Library Associates*. St. Cloud, MN: Sentinel Printing, 2002.

Hollingsworth .... Hollingsworth, Lloyd. *Gustavus Athletics: A Century of Building the Gustie Tradition, 1880–1980*. St. Peter: Gustavus Adolphus College, 1984.

Johnson, D. .... Johnson, Dennis J. *Esbj!: The Heart and Mind of a Professor*. Self-published, 2007.

Johnson, E. .... Johnson, Emeroy. *Eric Norelius: Midwest Pastor and Churchman*. Rock Island, IL: Augustana Book Concern, 1954.

Lund, *Celebrating* .. Lund, Doniver. *Gustavus Adolphus College: Celebrating 125 Years*. St. Peter: Gustavus Adolphus College, 1987.

Lund, *Centennial* ... Lund, Doniver. *Gustavus Adolphus College: A Centennial History, 1962–1962*. Minneapolis: Lund Press, 1963.

Norelius .... Norelius, Eric. *The Pioneer Swedish Settlements and Swedish Lutheran Churches in America, 1845–1860*. Rock Island, IL: Augusta Historical Society, 1984.

Peterson .... Peterson, Conrad. *Remember Thy Past: A History of Gustavus Adolphus College, 1862–1952*. Minneapolis: Brings Press, 1953.

INTERVIEWS
Almen Intv .... Almen, Jordan and Ted Almen. Interview by the author. August 27, 2010.

Davis Intv .... Davis, Nadvia. Interview by the author. April 21, 2011.

Frings Intv .... Frings, Sam. Interview by the author. December 15, 2010.

Getfield Intv .... Getfield, Kareen. Interview by the author. January 15, 2010.

Hanson Intv .... Hanson, Mark. Interview by the author. May 9, 2011.

Harms Intv .... Harms, Jenni. Interview by the author. November 16, 2010.

Larson Intv .... Larson, Ruth. Interview by the author. September 14, 2010.

Malmborg Intv .... Malmborg, John. Interview by the author. November 16, 2010.

Mikel Intv .... Mikel, Lainey. Interview by the author. December 8, 2010.

Mlynar Intv .... Mlynar, Kari. Interview by the author. December 15, 2010.

Squier Intv .... Squier, Lacey. Interview by the author. September 14, 2010.

Wasson Intv .... Wasson, Matthew. Interview by the author. September 3, 2010.

Wren Intv .... Wren, Linnea. Interview by the author. January 18, 2010.

ANCESTRY
1. Almen Intv; *Weekly,* January 12, 1926, October 7, 1947; Lund, *Centennial,* 114.
2. *GQ,* Fall 1956.
3. *Weekly,* October 2, 1992.

BENCHMARKS
1. *Weekly,* September 30, 1966, April 12, 1983; 1983 *Gustavian*.
2. Lund, *Celebrating,* 22.
3. *Weekly,* January 29, 1947.

CONVERSATION
1. *GQ,* Fall 2004, 15.
2. Ibid., 16.
3. Ibid.
4. Ibid., Summer 2004, 19.
5. Ibid., Summer 1996, 5.
6. Wren Intv.
7. *GQ,* Summer 1996, 7.
8. "Meet Lisa Heldke," http://admission.gustavus.edu/admissions/spotlight/spotlight.asp?iSpotID=315, accessed March 2, 2011.

[NOTES]

DON'T
1. Lund, *Centennial*, 53. (I have exercised a bit of creative license here, contracting Wahlstrom's original words, "do not," to conform with the chapter's title.)
2. *GQ*, October 1945, July 1961; 1935 *Gustavian*; Larson Intv.
3. Lund, *Celebrating*, 78.

ELEMENTS
1. *Weekly*, December 9, 1930.
2. Ibid., January 8, 1921; December 6, 1927.
3. Ibid., December 14, 1973.
4. *FN*, 1992–93, No. 1.

FAITH
1. *Weekly*, November 25, 1955.
2. Ibid., January 13, 1956.
3. Ibid., October 4, 1957.
4. Ibid., January 12, 1962.
5. *GQ*, Spring 1995.
6. Johnson, D., 49.
7. *GQ*, Summer 2003, 16.
8. Lund, *Centennial*, 40.
9. Ibid., 85.
10. *Weekly*, January 10. 1933.
11. Lund, *Centennial*, 41.
12. *Weekly*, April 28, 1988
13. *GQ*, Winter 2008, 18.

GROUPS
1. Squier Intv.
2. *GQ*, Summer 2005.
3. 1941 *Gustavian*.
4. *MST*, January 8, 1994.
5. *Weekly*, December 11, 1923.
6. Ibid., October 12, 1973.

HEADLINERS
1. Frings Intv.
2. *GQ*, February 1972, 7.

IDEALISM
1. Harms Intv; *Weekly*, November 5, 2010.
2. *Weekly*, May 8, 1970
3. Ibid., April 3, 1970; Barth, 63–67.

JOURNEY
1. Getfield Intv.
2. Ibid.
3. Ibid.

4. Kareen Getfield, online journal entry, September 21, 2010, https://gustavus.studioabroad.com/index.cfm?w=09%2F19%2F2010&jid=23873&FuseAction=Public.Journals, accessed June 14, 2011.
5. Getfield Intv.
6. *GQ*, December 1981, 6.
7. *Weekly*, September 17, 1929.
8. Ibid., February 11, 1947.
9. Ibid., February 15, 1938.
10. Ibid., March 13, 1981.
11. Ibid., February 23, 1974.
12. 1989 *Gustavian*.

KITCHENS
1. 1976 *Gustavian*; *GQ*, May 1977; *SPP*, March 23, 1977; *MST*, August 16, 1992.
2. *Weekly*, January 11, 1938.
3. Lund, *Centennial*, 53–54.
4. *Weekly*, March 3, 1950.

LANDMARKS
1. Lund, *Centennial*, 37–40; *Weekly*, October 25, 1921, November 2, 1926.
2. *SPP*, September 18, 2003.
3. *Weekly*, October 14, 1966.
4. *GQ*, November 1959.
5. Ibid., Spring 2003.
6. *Weekly*, November 22, 1996.

MORTARBOARDS
1. *Weekly*, November 8, 1921.
2. Lars P. Lundgren, "Gustavus Adolphus College, 1890–1925," in Campus Files/Commencement #2, GAC Archives.
3. *Weekly*, May 23, 1939.
4. 1965 *Gustavian*.
5. Barth, 24.
6 Elvee, 116.

NOTABLES
1. *Valkyria*, 1909; *GQ*, October 31, 1944, June 1951.
2. *Weekly*, January 29, 1971.
3. *GQ*, March 1947.

OCCASIONS
1. Mikel Intv.
2. *Weekly*, November 30, 1951.
3. 1974 *Gustavian*.

PERFORMANCE
1. *Weekly*, March 11, 1941, March 18, 1941; *GQ*, Spring 2003.

[NOTES]

QUARTERS
1. *Weekly*, September 25, 1946; *GQ*, October 1946, Summer 2005; Lund, *Centennial*, 125–26; Lund, *Celebrating*, 68–72.
2. *Weekly*, November 11, 1942.
3. *GQ*, Fall 2007, 29.

RESILIENCE
1. *SPP*, March 31, 1998, September 10, 1998, March 28, 1999; *Minneapolis Star Tribune*, October 22, 1998.
2. *SPP*, April 5, 1998.
3. *Weekly*, March 14, 2008.
4. Hollingsworth, 124–27.
5. Barth, 51.
6. Ibid., 62.
7. *GQ*, March 1970, 17.

STUDY
1. *Weekly*, December 10, 2010.
2. Mlynar Intv.
3. *Weekly*, January 19, 1962.
4. Ibid., October 25, 1974.

TOWN
1. Malmborg Intv.; *Weekly*, November 6, 1959.
2. *NOTA*, April 6, 1973.
3. *Weekly*, October 10, 1980.
4. *GQ*, Spring 2001, 10.
5. *MFP*, May 25, 1998.

US
1. Davis Intv.
2. Black Student Organization to "Prospective Freshman," July 30, 1976, GACA 236, Collection of the Black Student Organization, Box 15.5.3, Folder 14, GAC Archives.
3. *Weekly*, November 15, 1921.
4. *MT*, May 31, 1970.
5. *GQ*, Winter 2000, 8.
6. Axel Steuer, "An Uncommon Community," *FN*, 67, 1 (September 10, 1997), 11.

VARSITY
1. *GQ*, Summer 2003, 24–27; *Weekly*, March 28, 2003; *SPP*, March 23, 2003.
2. Mike Dickens to Mark Hanson, undated, GAC Sports Information files.
3. Hanson Intv.

WELCOME
1. Wasson Intv.
2. *Weekly*, October 10, 1958.
3. Ibid., September 19, 1958.
4. Ibid., May 27, 1960.
5. GACA 156, Collection of Tau Mu Tau Sorority, Box 4, GAC Archives.

X CHROMOSOMES
1. *Weekly*, May 18, 1926.
2. Ibid., May 6, 1941.
3. Ibid., September 30, 1955.
4. Ibid., September 29, 1983.
5. Ibid., September 24, 2010.
6. Ibid., March 18, 2005.

Y CHROMOSOMES
1. *Weekly*, May 18, 1926.
2. Ibid., October 23, 1920; April 28, 1925.
3. Ibid., April 22, 1940.

ZEITGEIST
1. Bethany College in Lindsborg, Kansas, shared the "Rockar Stockar" cheer with Gustavus and still uses it today to root on its teams, known as the "Terrible Swedes." Bethany College Web Site http://www.bethanylb.edu/traditions.html, accessed February 3, 2011.
2. Larson Intv.; *Weekly*, October 3, 1922.
3. *Weekly*, September 27, 1944.
4. Ibid., December 13, 1968.
5. Ibid, December 13, 1974.
6. Ibid, October 31, 1985.

Å, Ä, Ö
1. *Weekly*, November 8, 1932.
2. Johnson, E., 190.
3. Peterson, 59.
4. Lund, *Centennial*, 145.
5. Johnson, E., 190.
6. *SPP*, April 10, 1976.
7. *GQ*, July 1974, 12.

Guess that Gustie!

Peter Krause '87 — Television actor (*Six Feet Under; Parenthood*)

Linda Gulder Huett '66 — Former president and CEO of Weight Watchers International

Kevin Kling '79 — Storyteller and essayist

Allison Rosati '85 — News anchor, WMAQ-TV, Chicago

Barbara Andrews '58 — First ALC woman pastor

Magnus Ranstorp '85 — Internationally renowned expert on terrorism and counter-terrorism

ILLUSTRATION CREDITS

GUSTAVUS ADOLPHUS COLLEGE ARCHIVES

6 (Alexis P-22); 7 (strip P-02482-04; classroom P-5182; report cards P-6484); 8 (summer school P-5950; crowd P-03149); 9 (freshmen P-5978); 11 (physics P-3442; canteen P-5187); 12 (Forell P-466; Baumgartner P-233); 15 (chapel P-2255; skeleton P-3454; cow GACA0159-01-02-02); 16 (old car P-2269; sign P-2326); 17 (smoke P-5243); 18 (sled P-06482); 19 (Hello Walk P-4617; car P-4659; snow P2313-06; sled P-4655; Old Main P-1817); 20 (under tree P-2313-18; valley P-05641); 21 (rain P-2313-8; sunning P-2444-2); 22 (chapel P-2364-2); 23 (service P-6371; windows P-2377-1; Elvee P-6483); 25 (mural P-3411); 27 (train P-4611; 1903 debate P-6198; intl debate P-6197); 28 (aqua P-2571; KYSM P-4639); 29 (softball P-2150; powderpuff P-2065); 30 (*Weekly* P-4639); 33 (Nobel); 34 (Bryan P-4608); 35 (Merrill P-6562); 38 (Wilkie GACA 0159-01-02-03; vigil P-5190); 41 (Stevens P-2563); 42 (Wang GACA 0270-01-01; Gomez GACA 0159-01-02-01); 43 (Japanese P-5238); 45 (strip P-2675; Seven Gables P-7021; Kemp's P-7020; cooks P-5800); 46 (cooks P-5799; dining P3111); 49 (Hello Walk P-2300; book store P-2279; Granlund P-3173); 50 (water tower [both] P-6819; P-3156; rock painting P-2308-1); 51 (old sign P-5977); 52 (1890 class P-5949); 53 (roof GACA 0268-01-01; 1924 grads P-2545); 54 (speaker P-5980; procession P-5986; flags P-5985); 55 (1976 grads P-5988); 61 (Hallander P-2670); 62 (young Eberhart P-2634-01; young Levander P-6197); 63 (Magny P-997); 64 (Lucia [both] P-2622-1; P-2679); 65 (Christmas P-2386-01; Royal Affair [both] CAMC0020-03-35; CAMC0020-03-33); 66 ("Flush" P-06742; tires P-06741; queens P-2623); 67 (Hafdahl P-06791; May pole P-06489); 69 (choruses P-2738; piano P-04878); 70 (1961 choir P-2709; orchestra P-05277); 71 ("Wuthering" GACA0274-01-01-01: "Godspell" P-06105; "Impresario" P-05321); 72 (railers [both] P-2470; P-3182); 73 (Old Main P-2471; South P-3026-10; roomers P-05503; Johnson P-2418; Uhler P-2456-12); 74 (1900 room P-3232; 1938 room P-2466; 1941 room GACA0274-01-01-02; 1908 room P-2465); 75 (1904 women P-5504; 1930s room GACA0159-01-01-03; pyramid P-06207; bunk P-05791; shower P-04644); 76 (Old Main [by Glenn Kranking] CAMC0024-01-01-02); 77 (Lund [by Glenn Kranking] CAMC0024-01-01-01); 78 (bus P-3499; Myrum P-6238); 79 (fire P-2230-1; records P-2232; ruins P-2233); 81 (Old Main library P-3485; first F.B. library P-5433; second F.B. library P-04651); 82 (men's room P-3230; woman's room P-2579); 83 (Commerce P-3381; fireplace P-3091); 84 (library P-3357); 86 (Pizza Villa P-04766); 87 (Swanbeck's P-05517-03; Nicollet P-06892; Flame P-06893); 88 (St. Peter P-6810); 89 (window P-2278; parade P-1828; float P-06740; volunteers GACA0113-05-01-01); 91 (co-ed class P-05952; men lab P-3457; women lab P-3445); 93 (BSO GACA0236-04-04-02; Barth/Bryant P-2753); 95 (1920s football P-06431); 96 (hockey P-6283; gymnastics P-06282; track P-06430); 97 (Bees P-06266); 100 (arrival P-2316; hug P-04654); 101 (1920 reunion P-05856); 102 (tug-o-war P-5906); 104 (check-out P-04645); 105 (strip P-2070; bikes P-644; four women P-5552; eleven women P-5188); 106 (IBs GACA0265-01-02-01; TMTs GACA0156-03-04-03); 107 (Rec Assn P-2081; golf 2072); 108 (check-out P-04646); 109 (basketball P-06222; six men GACA0159-01-01-02); 110 (Grays [both] P-2582; P-2590; paddling GACA0274-01-01-03); 111 (Letterman GACA0159-01-01-01); 113 (Class of 1917 P-05948; band P-05278; three friends GACA0159-01-01-05; four friends GACA0159-01-01-04; around "Gus" P-3068); 114 (dancing GACA0110-03-01; skiers P-06484; four friends P-5141; courtyard P-2455); 115 (caf P-04647); 116 ("Gus" P-6564); 117 (Kilander P-2688; smorgasbord P-3134; Auditorium P-2248); 118 (archbishop P-2917); 119 (Wallenberg P-150)

GUSTAVUS ADOLPHUS COLLEGE OFFICE OF MARKETING AND COMMUNICATION

Credited

Anthony Adams: 99 (Ford)
Anders Bjorling: 20 (aspen); 65 (flutes)
Jen Fox: 27 (forensics)
Erin Fredrick: 41 (India)
Glenn Kranking: 77 (toppled spire)
Lindsay Lelivelt: 29 (broomball)
Edward Paul Macko: 13 (Wren)
Amy McMullan: 51 (new sign); 67 (banners)
Alex Messenger: 13 (Freiert); 16 (dance); 19 (strip); 25 (Proclaim); 37 (dancing); 69 (recital); 81 (G.A. sweatshirt); 89 (Nazario); 117 (Thorstensson)
John Noltner: 13 (Heldke); 53 (strip)
Tom Roster: v; 5 (Johnsons); 7 (professors); 11 (Easton); 55 (2008 grads; toss); 66 (royalty); 70 (saxophone; cello); 74 (2009 room); 93 (Building bridges; Asian); 99 (orientation [both]; candlelight); 100 (carry tubs); 101 (1988 reunion); 106 (Sigmas); 119 (new Swedish House)
Brittany Salisbury: 117 (strip)
Hanna Schutte: 11 (outdoors); 33 (Walcott); 41 (table)
Stacia Vogel: 13 (Lammert); 23 (Johnson); 47 (salad); 49 ("Gus"); 51 (spire [color]); 77 (service)
Steve Wolt: 97 (track); 115 (three friends)
SportsPix: 97 (soccer; swimming; Nordic; golf; women's hockey; women's tennis; baseball)

123

Clarence R. Magney 1903
Only Gustie to have a Minnesota state park named after him

Kurt Elling '89
Grammy-winning jazz vocalist

Patsy O'Connell Sherman '52
3M chemist and co-inventor of Scotchguard®

James McPherson '58
Pulitzer Prize-winning author of *Battle Cry of Freedom*

Ruth Youngdahl Nelson '24
1973 National Mother of the Year

Bill Holm '65
Poet and essayist

[ILLUSTRATION CREDITS]

Uncredited
3 (families); 4 (map; covers); 5 (Johns; Eckmans; Erdmans); 12 (Christensen; Lindemann); 17 (skateboard); 23 (postcard); 25 ("Faith"); 29 (hockey; dodgeball); 33 (Morrison); 34 (Davis; Ling); 35 (Johnson); 37 (Peace Corps); 39 (tabling); 41 (Peru); 49 (sculpture); 51 (cabin; spire [b&w]); 53 (procession P-5987; long and short P-1590; women P-5947); 67 (broomball); 68 (Grainger); 69 (China; bassoon); 70 (2009 choir); 71 (dancers); 73 (stadium); 78 (fieldhouse); 83 (laptop; arb); 88 (St. Ansgar's); 90 (Davis); 93 (Bryant; Diversity Center); 94 (team/fans); 105 (two women); 109 (cell phone); 111 (SAE); 115 (guitars); 118 (Bernadotte); king; prince; Von Sydow); 119 (Legaros)

GUSTAVUS SPORTS INFORMATION
61 (Lindquist); 95 (1902 football; baseball; basketball); 96 (swimming; basketball); 97 (men's hockey; gymnastics; men's tennis)

GUSTAVUS PUBLICATIONS
Gustavian Weekly (Various)
10 ("Conversation" 9/6/91); 14 ("Skoning's" 1/28/30); 35 (Ben Folds [photo morgue]); 38 (anti-war cartoon 1/21/41; "season" cartoon 10/15/65; long-hair cartoon 3/7/69); 39 (head cartoon 10/22/65; trees cartoon 4/3/70); 45 (ad 12/8/25); 46 (ad 2/15/49; cartoon 10/7/77); 50 (cartoon 10/14/66); 54 (ad 5/24/57); 78 (headline 11/15/38); 83 (cartoon 1/19/62); 86 (ad 4/8/60); 87 (Nutter ad 9/27/27; Flame ad 10/3/75); 92 (Easter 9/29/50; Patterson cartoon 3/18/55); 93 (logo 5/2/69)

Manhem (1904)
2 (Gustav); 70 (band); 88 (cartoon)

Valkyria (1909)
61 (seal)

Gustavian (Various)
2 (John 1950); 3 (Ted 1979); 5 (Ted 1961; Marietta 1962); 6 (PBK 1983); 7 (sleep 1969; 9 (home ec 1947; nurses 1963; Curriculum II 1989); 10 (Owen 1973); 14 (shack 1935); 15 (cartoon 1929); 16 (linger 1954; lawn 1963); 17 (drink 1973; clothes 1974); 24 (Ford 1931); 28 (senate 1952); 33 (strip 1964; Borlaug 1971; Wiesel 1994); 34 (Atlee 1959; Sandburg 1952); 35 (Smothers 1963; Mathis 1965; Denver 1971; Jardine 1974); 37 (cartoon 1931; Rosati 1987); 38 (march 1970); 39 (sign 1971; divest 1989); 41 (Stonehenge 1988); 42 (Magalee 1946; Jensen 1947; Selassie 1950; jukebox 1952; Bim/Jyrki 1954); 43 (Cosmo 1955); 46 ("food stinks" 1966); 50 (rock "breathe" 1986); 54 (Tang 1968; alternative 1971); 60 (Lawson 1931; Wingstrand cartoon 1922; Andreen cartoon 1917); 61 (Emil 1937; Barney 1971); 62 (young Youngdahl 1917); 63 (Youngdahl 1925; O'Connell 1952; Andrews; McPherson 1958; Holm 1965; Gulder 1966; Kling 1979; Rosati; Ranstorp 1985; Krause 1987; Elling 1989); 71 ("Menagerie" 1997); 74 (1951 room 1951); 75 (1973 women 1973; Co-ed sign 1971; cage 1968); 78 (Anderson; Olson 1941); 82 (cartoon 1925; bulb 1966); 87 (grill 1954); 91 (Andersons/Johnsons 1927); 92 (Towley 1925; Hobart 1935; Patterson 1955); 96 (football 1955); 99 (picnic 1959); 100 (dad 1961; wave 1958); 101 (hazing 1961; freshmen 1962; first-year women 1963); 106 ("Gay 90" 1952); 107 (ducky 1971); 109 (beards 1950; discus 1968); 110 (Alphs 1962); 111 (bust sign 1971; bartenders 1972; V-12 1944); 112 (basketball team 1931); 113 (V-12 1944); 114 (piano 1965); 115 (six friends 1995)

Gustavus Quarterly
4 (cartoon [Fall 1956]); 28 (sauna [Spring 1993]); 34 (Lee [Spring 1992]); 35 (Bergen [September 1950]); 44 (bread [March 1965]; Young ad [Fall 1992])

Gustavus Catalogs
8 ("Departments" [1890-91]); 15 (regulations [1885-86])

UNAFFILIATED HISTORICAL ARCHIVES
Minnesota Historical Society
7 (Ph.D.s); 29 (football); 62 (Lind; Eberhart portrait; Youngdahl portrait; Gov. Levander)

Nicollet County Historical Society
48 (Old Main); 50 (rocks)

INDIVIDUALS
Jeff Anderson: 43 (festival [both])
Erica Fernstrom: 93 (Queers)
Kareen Getfield: 40 (Getfield)
Bruce Gray: 92 (reunion)
Chris Johnson: 37 (key chains)
Erin Luhmann: 37 (Luhmann)
Byron Nordstrom: 119 (band; old Swedish House; door)
Barb Larson Taylor: 115 (four friends)

ORIGINAL PHOTOGRAPHY
Stan Waldhauser
7 (report cards); 8 (catalog); 24 (ribbon); 27 (ribbon); 36 (member tag); 45 (coupon book); 47 (Gustieware); 48 (spoon; plate); 52 (diploma); 53 (ring); 66 (buttons); 67 (button; poster); 68 (pins); 77 (pin; finial); 79 (plate); 82 (notebook); 95 (buttons); 96 (button); 98 (nametag); 101 (beanie); 106 (feather; garter); 108 (paddle); 116 (button); 117 (poster)

Dave Kenney
2 (couch); 18 (traying); 26 (Squier); 32 (Nestle); 36 (sleep-out); 47 (tomatoes); 64 (Mikel); 80 (Ohles); 107 (Womyn's); 111 (M-Pact); 112 (Larson)

Grace Kenney
98 (greeters)

INDEX

A

Å, Ä, Ö, 116–119
"A Royal Affair," fundraising event, 65
academic calendar, 9
academic standards, 6–9
Adolph (cartoon character), 60
Adolphus Jazz Ensemble, 70
Agan, Angie, 76
A.H. Anderson Social Science Center, 58
Ahlstrom, Millard, 14
Alexis, Gerhard, 6
Alfred Nobel Hall of Science, 33, 58
Almen, Gustav Theodore, 2
Almen, John, 2
Almen, Jordan, 2
Almen, Lars Gustav, 2
Almen, Ted, 2
Almen family, 2, 3
Almen-Vickner Guest House, 2
alumni, 62, 101
Alumni Association, 4
alumni records destroyed, 79
American Forensic Association National Individual Events Tournament, 27
Amundson, Hans, 15
"Amundson's Ko" (cow), 15
ancestry, 2–5
Anderson, Charles, 3
Anderson, Cindy, 71
Anderson, Cody, 3
Anderson, Donald V., 78
Anderson, Duncan, 3
Anderson, Esther, 91
Anderson, Paul, 86
Anderson, Raymond, 91
Anderson, Roger, 91
Anderson, Teri Carter, 3
Anderson, Tracey, 115
Anderson Fernstrom, Jeanenne, 3
Anderson Social Science Center, 81
Andreen, Franz Benjamin, 60
Andrews, Barbara, 63, 122
animal pranks, 15
anti-apartheid demonstration, 39
anti-war activities, 38
Arbor View Apartments, 59
Art Barn, 58
Arthur, Abner W., 58
Asfeld, Katie, 18
Asian Cultures Club, 93
Association of Women Students (AWS), 107

athletic equipment manager, 61
athletic stadium, 57, 59, 72–73
athletics, 27, 28–29, 94–97
Attlee, Clement, 34
Auditorium "Aud"
    building completed, 56
    chapel, 15, 22, 23, 117
    fire damage, 58, 79
autumn scenery, 20

B

"Babes," women's football team, 29
bands
    Jazz Lab Band, 70
    Proclaim Band, 25
    Symphony Band, 68, 70, 119
Barn, The, Le Sueur, 111
Barth, Frank, 39, 51, 54, 58, 79
Barth, Marge, 39
Bartoshuk, Linda, 32
baseball, men, 95, 96
basketball, men, 42, 44, 66, 94, 96, 97
basketball, women, 95, 112
Battey, Laurie, 41
Bauman, Mrs. J. A., 45
Baumgartner, Helen, 12
Beach Boys, 35
beard-growing contest, 109
benchmarks, 6–9
Beck, Donna Gabbert, 59
Beck, Warren, 59
Bergen, Edgar, 35
Bergstrand, J. L., 73
Bergstrom, Vern, 12
Bernadotte, Count Folke, 81, 118
Bernadotte, Countess Estelle, 118
Bertil, Prince of Sweden, 118
Big Hill Farm, 47
"Big Wheels," 99
Birgitta Singers, 70
Bittrich Johns, Marietta, 5
black and gold (school colors), 27
Black Student Organization (BSO), 90, 92, 93
black students, enrollment, 90–93
B&M Grill, 87
boarding department ("hash factory"), 45
Boise, David, 35
Bonn, Beverly, 46
Borlaug, Norman, 33
Brakke, Alex, 66

broomball, 29, 67
Brown, Nancy L. H., 23
Brudwick Kjellgren, Julie, 3
Bryan, William Jennings, 34
Bryant, Phil, 93
Building Bridges Conference, 40
Building Bridges student organization, 93
bus crash, 78

C

C. Charles Jackson Campus Center, 59
caf service. *See* food service
cafeteria, Student Union, 46
Cambridge University debates, 57
Campus Activities Board (CAB), 26, 37
campus canine, 61
Campus Center, 80
campus custodian, 61
campus police, 61
Canteen, 11
Carl XVI Gustaf, King of Sweden, 44, 118
Carlson, Edgar, 9, 17, 22, 24, 25, 34, 35, 54, 57, 92
Carlson, Inga, 58
Carlson, Ron, 12
Carlson International Center, 59
Carter Anderson, Teri, 3
Center for Student Leadership, 59
Center for Vocational Reflection, 111
Chamber Singers, 70
"Changing the World" J-Term class, 37
chapels, 22–23
Chi Iota Kappa fraternity, "Chieftains," 110
Chin Hsuan Wang, 42
Cho, Jim, 42
Choir of Christ Chapel, 70
choral groups, 69
Christ Chapel
    anti-apartheid (South Africa) demonstration, 39
    Christmas celebrations, 58, 65
    dedication, 22, 58
    groundbreaking (1959), 34
    new student orientation, 99
    "Sing-in for Peace," 38
    spire, 51
    St. Lucia celebration, 64
    student experiences, 23
    tornado damage, 76–77
Christenson, Ron, 12

[INDEX]

Christmas celebrations, 65
The Christy Minstrels, 33
civil rights movement, 38
Class of 1900, 53
Class of 1908, 53
Class of 1920, 101
Class of 1924, 53
Class of 1988, 101
Classroom Annex, 58
clothing, optional (streaking), 17
clothing styles, men students, 108
clothing styles, women students, 104
coasting, in snow, 18
Co-ed Hall (Norelius Hall), 2, 58, 75
Coleman, Eric, 90
College Avenue sign, 51
College brand, "Make Your Life Count," 59
College seal (1909), 60–61
College View Apartments, 59
commencement 1890, 52
Commencement 1900, 53
Commencement 1957, 54
Commencement 1961, 54
Commencement 1968, 54
Commencement 1971, 54
Commencement 1976, 55
Commencement 2008, 55
Commerce Building, 56
Commerce Hall library, 82
conversation, 10–13
Cosmopolitan Club, 43
curriculum
    4-1-4 academic calendar, 58
    overview, 8–9
    Swedish language, history, culture, 117
    Winter Term, 41
Curriculum II, 59
Curriculum II graduates, 9

D

Daly, Marty, 107
dance performances, 71
dance prohibition, 16
Dancing with the Profs, fundraising event, 37
Davis, Angela, 34
Davis, Bim, 42
Davis, Nadvia, 90
"Day of Involvement" (after Kent State shootings), 38

Dean, William, 10
death in campus community, 78
debate teams, 27
Delta Phi Omega sorority, 66, 106
Denver, John, 35
Dining Service. *See* food service
Diversity Center, 93
diversity in student population, 90–93
dodgeball, 29
don't (rules and regulations), 14–17
dormitories, 73–75
"Drama on Parade," radio program, 28
drinking prohibition, 17

E

early history of college, 48
East Union, second school, 22, 48, 56, 88
East Union Evangelical Lutheran Church, 22
Easter, Chuck, 92
Easton, Seán, 11
Eberhart, Adolph, 62
Eckhoff, Cecil, 79
Eckman family, 5
Eckman Mall, 26
Edgar M. Carlson Administration Building, 58
Edwin J. Vickner Hall of Language Arts, 58
elements, 18–21
Elling, Kurt, 63, 123
Ellwein, Steve, 51
Elvee, Richard, 23, 55
Emil (campus dog), 61
Engberg, Emmer, 24
Epsilon Pi Alpha fraternity, "Eppies," 110
Erdman, Judy Lund, 5
Esbjornson, Robert, 23, 114
ethnic heritage, 117
extracurricular activities, 27

F

faculty, impact on students, 11–12
fair trade activists, 39
faith, 22–25
Falk, Wally, 4
families, multi-generational connections, 2–5
Fernstrom, Erica, 3
Fernstrom, Gaylord, 3
Fernstrom, Jeanenne Anderson, 3

finals week, 80
fine arts, 68–71
fire disasters, 79
first graduates, 8, 52, 56
first intercollegiate football game, 56
first school, Red Wing, 22, 48, 56, 88
First Term Seminars (FTSs), 36
Flame Bar, 87
Folds, Ben, 35
Folke Bernadotte Memorial Foundation, 58
Folke Bernadotte Memorial Library, 25, 58, 65, 81, 84–85
food service, 44–47, 86
Food Service Building, 58
football, men, 57, 66, 78, 95, 96
football, women, 29, 57
Ford, Jamie, 99
Forell, George, 12
forensics program, 27
Fowler, Cary, 32
fraternities, 66, 110–111
"Fraternity Initiation Night," 50
fraternity precursors, 57
Freiert, Will, 13
Friberg, Daniel, 24
Frick, William K., 8
Frings, Sam, 32
Frodeen, John, 56
Frost Weekend, 67, 109
fundraising events
    "A Royal Affair" (Gustavus Library Associates benefit), 65
    Campus Activities Board, 37
    Dancing with the Profs, 37
    Evelyn "Ma" Young, 44
F.W. Olin Hall, 59

G

"G" Club, 111
Gabbert Beck, Donna, 59
Gamelin, Frank, 79
Getfield, Kareen, 40
G.I. bulge, 72
The Glass Menagerie (1997), 71
Godspell (1980), 71
golf, 96, 107
Gomez, Filiberto, 42
"Good Guys," 99
Grainger, Percy, 68
Granlund, Paul, sculptures, 49

[INDEX]

Gray, Bruce, 92
Grays (limited membership society), 57, 110
Greater Gustavus Association, 4
"Greeter Christmas," 98
Gregory, Don, 25, 51
groups, 26–31
Grubb, Sally, 97
Guess that Gustie!, 63
Guittar, Renee, 47
Gulder Huett, Linda, 63, 122
"Gus" (bust of King Gustavus Adolphus), 49, 57, 116
Gus (cartoon character), 60
Gustavian Weekly staff, 30–31
Gustavus Adolphus College Arboretum (Linnaeus Arboretum), 51, 58, 76
Gustavus Adolphus Symphony Band, 68, 70, 119
Gustavus Aquatic League, 28
Gustavus Athletics Hall of Fame, 58
Gustavus Choir, 70
Gustavus Dining Service, 18, 43. *See also* food service
Gustavus do's and don'ts, 1885 edition, 15
Gustavus Jazz Lab Band, 70
Gustavus Library Associates, 6, 58, 65
Gustavus Philharmonic Orchestra, 70
Gustavus Quarterly, 4
Gustavus Sauna Society, 28
Gustavus Symphony Orchestra, 69, 70
Gustavus Wind Orchestra, 70
Gustie cheer, 112
Gustie Gear, 104
Gustie Greeters, 98, 99
Gustie Rouser, 99
Gustieware, 47
Gymnasium, 56
gymnastics, 58, 96, 97

H

Haack, Dale, 17
Habitat for Humanity volunteers, 37
Haesecke's clothing store, 108
Hafdahl, Jaynice, 67
Haitian earthquake benefit, 37
Hallander, Ernest, 61
Halloween week (1934), 14
Hamrum, Charles, 10
Hansen, Sara, 41

Hanson, Bob, 73
Hanson, Brad, 114
Hanson, Lillian, 44
Hanson, Mark, 94
Harms, Brent, 3
Harms, Cathy Villars, 3
Harms, Jenni, 36
Harms, Jennifer, 3
Harms, Kelsey, 3
"hash factory" (boarding department), 45
Hauskens, Don, 96
Hawkins, Natasha, 105
headliners, 32–35
Heating Plant, 58
Heavies," women's football team, 29, 57
Hegstrom, Victor, 7
Heldke, Lisa, 13
Hello Walk, 49
Hilary, Frederic, 68
Hobart, Claire, 92
hockey, 29, 96, 97
Hollingsworth Field and Stadium, 57, 59, 72–73
Holm, Bill, 54, 63, 123
Holteus house, St. Peter, 73
home economics program, 9
homecoming, 66, 101, 117
homelessness seminar, 36
Honors Day, 6, 67, 69
House of Seven Gables boarding club, 45
Huett, Linda Gulder, 63, 122

I

idealism, 36–39
The Impresario (1956), 71
Independent Blessings, "IBs" (limited-membership literary society), 56, 106
initiation events, first-year students, 98–103
intercollegiate sports, 56, 57, 58, 59, 94–97
Intercultural Education program, 41
international athletic tournament, 42
International Center, 119
International Cultures Club, 43
international debates, 57
International Festival, 43
international students, 42–43
intramural sports (IMs), 29
Involvement Fair, 26
Iota Beta sorority, 106

J

Jackson, Andrew, 56
Jardine, Al, 35
Jensen, Erick, 42
Jodock, Darrell, 24
Johns, Marietta Bittrich, 5
Johns, Theodore, 5
Johns family, 5
Johns Family Courtyard, 5
Johns-Bittrich family, 5
Johnson, Amy, 82
Johnson, Anna, 44
Johnson, Brian, 23, 77
Johnson, Dennis J., 59
Johnson, Katelyn, 5
Johnson, Kelly Rome, 5
Johnson, Michael, 35
Johnson, O. J., 24, 57
Johnson, Pearl, 91
Johnson, Raymond, 91
Johnson, Victoria, 91
Johnson Hall, 45, 57, 73
Jones, Virgil, 90
Jordan, Harley, 61
journey, 40–43
Jurgenson, Kay, 37

K

Kansai University, Japan, 43
Kappa Sigma Chi fraternity, "Sigs," 110
Kemp's boarding club, 45
Kendall, John S., 25, 58
KGSM radio station, 26
Kilander, Karl, 15, 18, 117
"Kilander's Tupp" (rooster), 15
King, Talmadge, 93
kitchens, 44–47
Kjellgren, Grace, 3
Kjellgren, Julie Brudwick, 3
Kjellgren, Steve, 3, 47
Klammeus, Eva, 43
Kling, Kevin, 63, 122
Knight, Jim, 96
Knock, Ruth, 116
Knudson, Marjorie, 104
Knutson, Dick, 99
Koehler, Gretchen, 20
Krause, Peter, 63, 122
Kvanli, Machell, 66
KYSM radio studio, 28

[INDEX]

L

Ladies' Summer Sewing School, 8
Lammert, John, 13
landmarks, 48–51
Langkos, Judy, 100
Lanham, Barney, 61
Larson, Amy, 3
Larson, Anna, 3
Larson, Frank, 3
Larson, Jennifer Strand, 3
Larson, Joshua, 7
Larson, Karl, 11
Larson, Rachel, 64
Larson, Ruth Snyder, 112
Larson, William, 3
Lautz, Steve, 115
Lawson, Eben E., 15, 60, 82
"Leans," women's football team, 29, 57
Lee, Spike, 34
Legeros, Alex, 119
Legeros, Nicholas, 49
Leitch, Richard, 36
Levander, Harold, 62
Levis, Bill, 10
libraries, 80–83
Lie Aan Tan, 54
Lind, John, 62
Lindell, Edward A., 58
Lindemann, J. W. R., 12
Lindquist, Gus, 89
Lindquist, Jill, 58
Lindquist, Willie, 61
Ling, Lisa, 34
lingering prohibition, 16
Link (Gibbs Hall), 58
Linnaeus Arboretum, 51, 58, 76
Linner Lounge, Student Union, 82
Love, Mike, 35
Lucast, Erika, 12
Lucia Singers, 70
Luhmann, Erin, 37
Lund, Doniver, 14
Lund Arena, 32, 44, 59
Lund Center, 59
Lund Erdman, Judy, 5
Lunden, Walter, 57
Lundgren, Lars P., 52
Lutheran Church, GA relationship with, 24
Lutheran Minnesota Conference, 22
Lutheran Student Association (LSA), 22
Lyric men's chorus, 69

M

Magalee, John, 42
Magney, Clarence R., 63, 123
Make Your Life Count, 59
Malmborg, John, 86
Manhem (yearbook), 88
Market Place food court, 47, 80
Mason, Charles, 51
Mathis, Johnny, 35
Mattson, Peter, 15, 24, 56
Mauston, Callie, 3
Mauston, Casey, 3
Mauston, Jeff, 3
Mauston, Lynn Regli, 3
May Day festivals, 67
MAYDAY! Conference, 67
McCarthy, Charlie (ventriloquist's dummy), 35
McGregor, Heather, 64
McInerny, Mike, 96
McKnight, Roger, 117
McPherson, James, 63, 123
Melva Lind Interpretive Center, 59
men students, 108–111
men's athletics
    baseball, 95, 96
    basketball, 42, 44, 66, 94, 96, 97
    football, 57, 66, 78, 95, 96
men's organizations, 110–111
Merrill, Robert, 35
The Merry Wives of Windsor (1964), 71
Midnight Express, 80
Mikel, Lainey, 64
Minnesota Conference of the Lutheran Augustana Synod, 24, 48, 56, 95
Minnesota governors, 62
"Missionary Ford," 24
Mlynar, Kari, 80
"Mom's rye bread," 44
Morrison, Toni, 33
mortarboards, 52–55
move-in day, first-year students, 98, 100
M-Pact, 111
mural, Folke Bernadotte Memorial Library, 25
music and musicians, 68–71
Myrum, George B., 42, 57, 78
Myrum Memorial Fieldhouse, 57, 72, 78

N

National Interfraternity Conference., 111
Nazario, Sonia, 89
Nelson, Hilding "Skoning," 14
Nelson, Jocko, 29
Nelson, Justin, 4
Nelson, Kelly, 41
Nelson, Mildred, 116
Nelson, Russell, 24
Nelson, Ruth Youngdahl, 63, 123
Nelson Zanders, Lucy, 90
Nestle, Marion, 32
New Academic Building, 59
New Gymnasium (O.J. Johnson Student Union), 57
Nicollet County Draft Board, 38
Nicollet Hotel, 87
Nilsson, Henrick, 43
Nobel Conferences, 32, 33, 58
Nobel Foundation, 33
Nordstrom, Byron, 117
Norelius, Eric, 8, 24, 48, 56, 88, 116, 117
Norelius Hall (Co-ed Hall), 2, 58, 75
Norelius parking lot, [snow]driftmobiles, 19
North Hall, 56, 73
notables, 60–63
Nu Upsilon Gamma fraternity, 110
nursing program, 9, 58
Nutter's clothing store, 108
Nyquist, Jonas, 56

O

occasions, 64–67
O'Connell Sherman, Patsy, 63, 123
off-campus parties, 111
Ogden P. Confer Hall, 59
Ogren-Dehn, Sophia, 18
Ohle, Jack R., 25, 59, 80, 99, 111
Ohle, Kris, 80
O.J. Johnson Student Union, 46, 57, 82
Old Main
    cafeteria, 45
    dedication of, 116
    early history, 48, 56
    hill sloping from, 18
    library, 81
    pre-graduation breakfast
    steps, 19
    student housing, 73
    tornado damage, 76–77
"Old Mares," women's football team, 29
Olson, Carl, 78

[INDEX]

"Olympian Council" (limited-membership debating society), 57
Omega Kappa fraternity, "OKs," 110
Onkka, Joan, 64
opera, 71
oratorical contest, 56
oratory teams, 27
orchestral groups and activities, 69, 70
organic farm, 47
orientation, first-year students, 98–103
outdoor recreation, 18–21
Owen, Larry, 10, 12
Oxford University debates, 27, 57
Ozolins, Karl, 81

P
Parents' Weekend, 46
parking prohibition, 16
Patrick's bar, 87
Patterson, Bill "Shorty," 92
Peace Corps volunteers, 37
peace strike, 38
performance, 68–71
Perish, Patrick, 18
Peterson, Conrad, 7, 62
Peterson, Ella, 69
Peterson, James L., 59
Phi Alpha fraternity, "Alphs," 110
Phi Beta Kappa chapter, 6, 59
philanthropy, Alumni Association, 4
Pi Kappa Delta national championship, 27
Pittman Hall (Valley View Hall), 58
Pittman residence hall, 98
Pizza Villa, 86
powderpuff football, 29
Prairie View Hall, 59
"pre-fabs" (student housing), 72
President's Banquet, 99
President's Christmas Dinner, 117
President's House (White House), 56, 58
Proclaim Band, 25

Q
quarters, 72–75
Queers & Allies student organization, 93

R
Raarup, Denny, 61
Ranch House (student housing), 57, 72
Ranstorp, Magnus, 63, 122
"Reading in Common," 89, 99
recruitment of minority students, 90–93

Red Wing, first school, 22, 48, 56, 88
Redeen, Bob, 53
Reds (limited membership society), 57, 110
Reedstrom, Lloyd, 113
Reformation Day (October 31, 1876), 48
Regli Mauston, Lynn, 3
religion, 22–25
relocation proposal, 56
resilience, 76–79
Roberts, Don, 96
rock(s) (landmarks), 50
Rome Johnson, Kelly, 5
Rosati, Allison, 63, 122
Rundstrom girls, 16
Rundstrom Hall, 18, 34, 57, 73
Rusesabagina, Paul, 40

S
St. Ansgar's Academy, East Union, 48, 56, 62, 88
St. Ansgar's Chorus, 70
St. Lucia celebration, 64
St. Peter
    Armory, 72
    businesses, 108
    relationship with GA, 86–89
    third school, 22, 48, 56
    water tower, 50
"St. Peter Reads," 89
Sandburg, Carl, 34
"save the trees" protest, 39
Scandinavian Area Studies, 117
Schaefer Fine Arts Center, 58
school colors, 27
school name, 56
school sign on College Avenue, 51
school songs, 27
Schueffner, Matt, 66
Schumann women's chorus, 69
second school, East Union, 22, 48, 56, 88
secret societies, 110
Seibel, Jeanette, 2
Selassie, Seifu, 42
Service of Nine Lessons and Carols, 65
shack-tipping incident, 14
Sherman, Patsy O'Connell, 63, 123
Sigma Alpha Epsilon fraternity (SAE), 111
Sigma Sigma Sigma sorority, 106
Simon, Erin, 18

Sisson, Donald, 22
skateboarding prohibition, 17
smoking prohibition, 17
Smothers Brothers, 35
Snyder Larson, Ruth, 112
soccer team, 58
Söderblom, Nathan, 118
softball, 29
Sohre Hall, 58, 98
Sorensen Hall, 58
Sorenson, Niels, 42
sororities, 66, 106
sorority precursors, 56
South Hall, 56, 73
Southwest Hall, 59
spirit yells, 27
Sponberg Young, Evelyn "Ma," 17, 44, 86, 112
sports
    intercollegiate, 56, 57, 58, 59, 94–97
    intramural (IMs), 29
    men, 42, 44, 57, 66, 78, 94, 95, 96, 97
    women, 28, 29, 57, 58, 59, 95, 97, 107, 112
Springston, Jerry, 37
Squier, Lacey, 26
stadium, 57, 59, 72–73
Steen, Tyron, 87
Steuer, Alex, 76
Steuer, Axel, 59, 93
Stevens, George, 41
Strand, Adam, 9
Strand, Tim, 77
Strand Larson, Jennifer, 3
streaking, 17
student activists, 39
student dormitories, 73
student housing, 72–75
student pacifists, 38
student pranks, 14–17, 50
student protests, 38, 39
Student Senate, 28
Student Union, 46, 57, 82
students
    diversity, 90–93
    men, 108–111
    women, 104–107
students with physical disabilities, 92
study, 80–85
study abroad programs, 40, 41, 119
Suderman, Elmer, 21

129

[INDEX]

Susan Kranz, 104
Swanbeck's Restaurant, 87
Swanson, Albert, 58
Swanson Tennis Center, 59
Swedberg's Drug Store, 87
Swedish connections, 116–119
Swedish dignitaries, visits, 118
Swedish House, 119
Swedish Lutheran Church, Red Wing, 22, 48, 56, 88
swimming, 58, 96
Sydow, Max Von, 118
Sylvia, Queen of Sweden, 118

T

Tau Mu Tau sorority, 106
Tau Psi Omega fraternity, 66, 110
tennis, 59, 96, 97
The Barn, *see* Barn, The
theatre performances, 71
third school, St. Peter, 22, 48, 56
Thorson, Bruce, 37
Thorson, Jerry, 12
Thorstensson, Roland, 117
Three Crowns Room, 32
timeline, 56–59
TMT, "The Modest Ten," "The Modest Tribe" (limited-membership literary society), 56, 106
tornado (1998), 59, 76–77, 89
Towley, Louis, 92
town, 86–89
track and field, 96
tragedies and disasters, 76–79
"Trailer Town" (student housing), 72
traying, in snow, 18
"Turbescon," "T.C.O.S.", 110
Tuukanan, Jyrki, 42

U

Uhler, Jacob, 57
Uhler Hall
    building completed, 57, 73
    cafeteria, 46, 86
    dining room, 46
    student pranks, 14
us (student demographics), 90–93
U.S. Navy V-12 training unit, 57, 111

V

Valkyria, 60
Valley View Hall (Pittman Hall), 58
varsity (sports), 94–97
Vasa Wind Orchestra, 70
Vickner Hall, 2
Villars Harms, Cathy, 3
volleyball, 97
volunteerism, 36–37

W

Wahlstrom, Matthias, 14, 52, 56, 91
Wahlstrom Hall, 58
Walcott, Derek, 33
Wallenberg, Linda, 119
Wasson, Matthew "Chooey," 98
welcome events, first-year students, 98–103
Wenaas, Julie, 115
Wettergren, Bob, 89
Whiskey River bar, 87
Wiesel, Elie, 33
Wilkie, Wendell, 38
Wilkins, Terena, 80
Wilkinson, Steve, 97
Winfield, O. A., 7, 57
Wingstrand, Evelyn, 60
women students, 104–107
Women's Athletic Association, 107
women's athletics
    basketball, 95, 112
    football, 29, 57
    golf, 107
    gymnastics, 58
    varsity, 97
Women's Center, 107
women's chorus, 69
women's organizations, 106–107
Women's Recreation Association, 107
Women's Referral Service, 107
Womyn's Awareness Center, 107
Wood, Eric, 5
Wren, Linnea, 13

X

X chromosomes, 104–107

Y

Y chromosomes, 108–111
Yost, Anna, 18
Young, Evelyn "Ma" Sponberg, 17, 44, 86, 112
Young, Gus, 44
Youngdahl, Luther, 62
Youngdahl Nelson, Ruth, 63, 123
Youngquist, W. R., 116

Z

Zanders, Lucy Nelson, 90
Zanders, Otis, 90
zeitgeist, 112–115